HADRIAN'S VILLA

Texts by
Benedetta Adembri

Ministero per i Beni e le Attività Culturali
Soprintendenza Archeologica per il Lazio

HADRIAN'S VILLA

Electa

Cover
Hadrian's Villa, The Canopus

Translation
Eric De Sena

Reprint 2004
First Edition 2000

An editorial realization Mondadori Electa S.p.A., Milan

www.electaweb.it

Contents

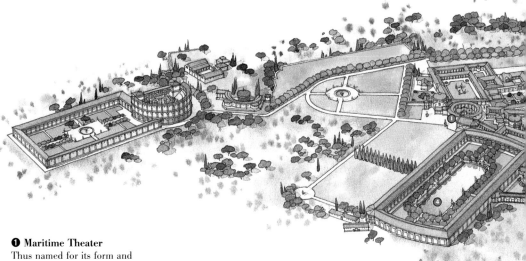

❶ Maritime Theater

Thus named for its form and decoration inspired by marine themes, this is a circular space with a diameter of about 25 meters that is surrounded by a canal. The theater was reached by means of two portable bridges, which were later substituted by a permanent cement structure.

❷ Piazza d'Oro

This is a peristyle (porticoed courtyard) with a central pool and small gardens. The short ends faced the Vestibule to the north and a polygonal space to the south. The Piazza d'Oro is among the largest areas within Hadrian's Villa. It was probably used by Hadrian to receive his court and diplomats.

❸ Building with Three

Exedras

This chamber was probably a *coenatio*, namely a dining room. The central space is rectangular, but beyond the colonnade three of the four walls were characterized, on the exterior, by semicircular apses embellished by porticoes; the northern wall was substituted by a monumental fountain.

❹ Pecile

A massive courtyard surrounded by four porticoes. 232 meters long and 97 meters wide, its short ends were curved. The central water pool is 106 meters long and 26 meters wide. The north side was originally a *porticus miliaria*, a portico, the length of which was planned according to the duration of after-dinner strolls advised by doctors.

❺ The Baths

Of modest proportions, the Small Baths were arranged around a central octagonal space that was illuminated by large windows. The Grand Baths were larger, but from an architectural point of view the plan was less experimental. One of the most notable areas of the baths was the *frigidarium*.

❻ Canopus

The elongated pool located at the center of this area was intended to mimic the canal that led from the city of Alexandria to Canopus, a city set on the Nile delta: hence the name of the complex. A large exedra (with a diameter of 15 meters) linked the pool to the adjacent areas.

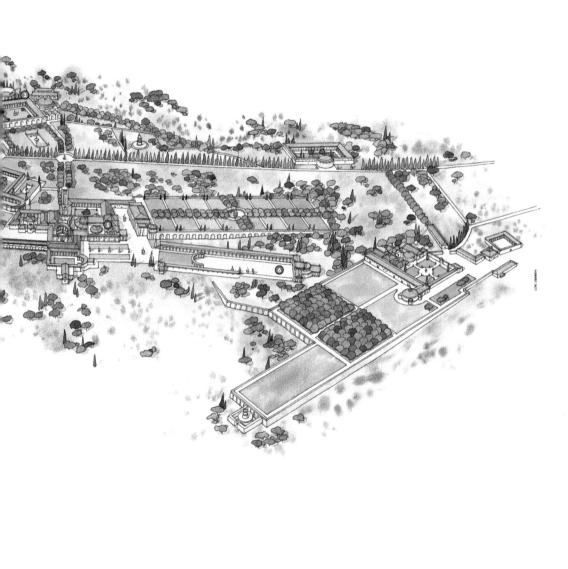

Hadrian

Hadrian's family tree.

Publius Aelius Hadrianus born in AD 76, probably in Italica (near modern-day Seville), to a family originally from Hadria in Piceno which had moved to Spain in the region of Baetica. Following the premature death of his father, Hadrianus Afer, cousin of Trajan, Hadrian was taken under the latter's wing (Trajan was childless) and raised in his home. Always beside the emperor, Hadrian enjoyed a successful military career, demonstrating a particular aptitude in the use of weaponry and in planning military operations; so talented was he that Hadrian assumed the rank of Major in the army (AD 101–102). He was later nominated as a member of the plebeian tribune, became a praetor and eventually a governor: first in Pannonia (AD 107) and later, in AD 114 or 117, in Syria. In fact, Hadrian was stationed in Antioch when he received word of Trajan's death (AD 117) and the election which made him emperor. His ascension to the throne was not without controversy: the fact that he was to assume the highest position of the state and especially because he had gained the favor of Trajan's wife Plotina, who, it was rumored, had been his lover and guided him in the choice of his own wife, did not save him from having to make a compromise with the Senate and increase the number of legions in order to maintain control of the army, which was so closely tied to his predecessor. We

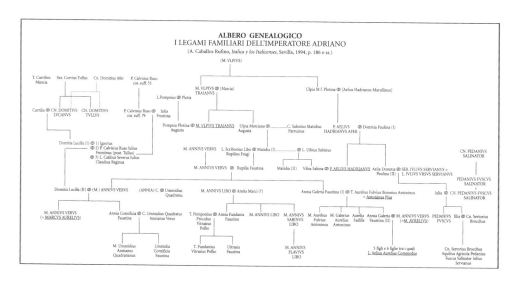

8

know that in 118, while Hadrian was in the area of the Danube organizing his defenses against the Sarmatians, a plot against him was discovered that had been planned by one of Trajan's most faithful military officials. It is certain, however, that even at the moment when Hadrian was officially adopted by Trajan and was simultaneously elected emperor, proclaimed by the widow just a few days after Trajan's death, there were suspicions that the entire process had been staged in an underhanded manner. Hadrian had surely been preparing to succeed Trajan for some time. He constantly tried to please the Trajan in many ways, modifying his behavior as he saw fit; for example, he only drank wine to satisfy the emperor.

The unquestionable qualities of his personality, which his contemporaries had already noticed, and in particular, his high level of intelligence, together with a notably strong will, were certainly factors that led to his achieving the objectives that he had set out to accomplish; in fact, there is an anecdote according to which the future emperor was injured by the ridicule thrown at him when the twenty-five year old had to deliver a public speech— he probably felt inferior because of his provincial upbringing and immediately set his mind to study Latin and became a master of the language in a very brief period of time. He was so gifted that a few years later, after the death of Lycinius Sura, Hadrian assumed the role of Trajan's official speech writer. Around AD 100 Hadrian married Vibia Sabina, daughter of Trajan's niece, Matidia, probably suggested by Plotina, but the marriage was not very serene: it is true that Sabina, according to the role that she was supposed to hold, accompanied the emperor on his official voyages, but Hadrian finally proclaimed that if he were a common citizen, he would have sought a divorce from his wife; he, in fact, drove the prefect of the Praetorian Guard under Trajan, Septicius Clarus, and the historian Suetonius Tranquillus, his secretary, away from Rome, accusing them of having overstayed their welcome in his home while he was absent. In reality, this conjugal strife should be examined in light of political

Portrait of Hadrian, Vaison-la-Romaine.

Bust of Hadrian,
from Italica (Baetica).
Seville, Archaeological
Museum.

motivations: Sabina had gathered a circle of traditionalist exponents, who made up her personal court and who Hadrian watched with great suspicion; perhaps he feared the prospect of internal opposition. Not even Sabina's death in AD 137 occurred without having an effect on the emperor's image: he was accused of having murdered his wife. Certainly this accusation allows us to understand how unpopular the emperor had become in the eyes of the populace, especially in the latter years of his reign and which led to him dying alone in Baia (AD 138). Not having any sons, he adopted Antoninus Pius just prior to his death. Antoninus Pius found no difficulty in securing the honor of divination for Hadrian, but provoked great bitterness among the senators.

In terms of Hadrian's character, the richest source of information is the biography attributed to Helius Spartianus, *Vita Hadriani*, in the collection of emperors' lives known as *Scriptores Historiae Augustae* from the 4th century AD: this was based largely upon the material in the autobiography that the emperor wrote himself, even though he wished not to divulge the name of the author, as well as other sources that did not always present favorable images of Hadrian. The use of so many sources resulted in a number of inconsistencies and contradictions among the information reported. The sources describe him as having been tall, robust and elegant in manner, with fine, manageable hair and, in stark contrast to all previous emperors, a beard. He led a frugal lifestyle, perhaps influenced by the many years spent on tiring military campaigns, where he demonstrated courage, audacity and the capacity to assess contingent situations in a manner whereby the best decisions were always reached. He was a passionate hunter, a sport he practiced his entire life, and did not hesitate to put his own life at risk. Enamored with Greek culture, he was called *graeculus*, Hadrian was well educated and possessed a phenomenal memory which allowed him to easily learn arithmetic and geometry, literature and art. In fact, he was both a writer and an artist; he wrote poetry and painted.

The versatility of his complex personality even included architecture, an art in which he enthusiastically immersed himself; he planned buildings with unusual designs, characterized by vaulted ceilings: this is confirmed by an anecdote regarding disputes he had with Trajan's official architect, Apollodorus of Damascus, who heavily criticized Hadrian's domes, defining them as "pumpkins." When Hadrian became emperor, Apollodorus was condemned to death as a result of his imprudent comments.

Contemporary literary sources define him as prodigious and avaricious, tolerant and irascible, very approachable to common people, yet often touchy and fickle with his friends. The unpredictable nature of his personality that emerges from this portrait of him, which stresses the difficulty he had in maintaining relationships with others, is confirmed by the words of the rhetorician Fronto. Writing to Marcus Aurelius, he identifies the cause of his extremely prudent behavior during the reign of Hadrian, as

Map of the Empire under Hadrian.

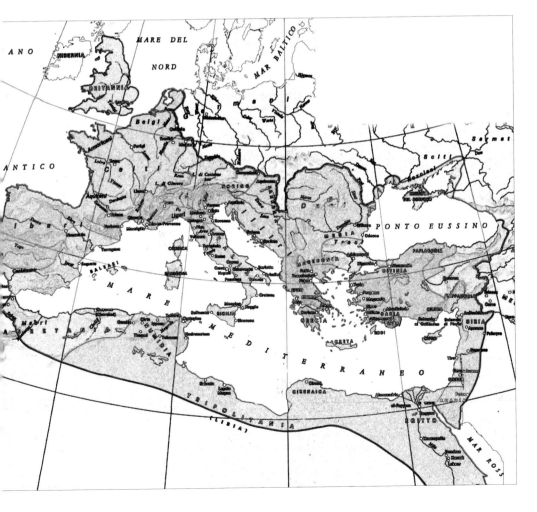

having owed to his fear of displeasing the emperor.

On the other hand, we know of Hadrian's political activities through the work that he conducted, attested by numerous commemorative inscriptions as well as through the representations and epigraphy on coins minted during his reign. As soon as he entered Rome for the first time as emperor in 118, he initiated a series of financial reforms, deeming it important to intervene in the affairs of the ruling class, with a change of blood in the top levels. Thus, he nominated new functionaries and dealt directly with the provinces in order to control the situations personally. He took judicial administration to heart, so much so that he sought the collaboration of an expert jurist, Salvius Julianus, in order to construct a new code of law, taking care not to neglect any aspect of life, as, for example, the improvement of the conditions of slaves. Despite his abilities in battle, Hadrian's politics were essentially directed toward the reestablishment of peace, and away from the expansionist trends of the Trajanic period, which compelled the Empire to exist in a constant state of warfare. One of his principal missions was to consolidate the borders of the Empire and, thus, was present along the Danube and the Rhine, where he reorganized the army and constructed impressive defenses, that he wished to oversee himself; in Britain he constructed the famous defense wall at the border with Scotland, while in the East, he preferred to withdraw from many areas, including Armenia, Mesopotamia and Assyria, areas in which the Romans were never able to establish stable rule. He attempted to establish friendly relationships with the Parthians and generally avoided repressive tactics, except in the case of Judea, where he reasserted order by extinguishing a revolt through bloodshed and by stripping autonomy from the province, which was consolidated into Syria. The emperor paid close attention to nurturing the provinces, improving and securing communication routes, and increasing the number of ports and cities, in order to stimulate commerce and facilitate the circulation of people belonging to different cultures: in this way, the Empire acquired a kind of unity that went beyond multiethnic composition and enjoyed a flourishing economy that involved a great amount of autonomy at the provincial level. In addition to this political economy, Hadrian, perhaps driven by the fact that he, himself, felt "provincial," sought to improve the physical appearance and the functionality of the cities, through the construction of gymnasia, temples, schools, shops and fountains, which rendered the places more livable. He especially favored the Greek-speaking cities (he, himself, spoke and wrote this language, even on official occa-

Hadrian's Travels

The novel political course, characterized by the particular attention Hadrian paid to events and financial administration in the provinces, justified, at least partially, the long periods of time in which he was absent from Rome. Such voyages were dictated, in the first place, by the need to personally oversee what was happening in the various parts of the Empire: Hadrian evidently deemed it necessary to be present in these areas in order to guarantee the stability of power over foreign peoples and lands, which he sought to obtain without the need to conduct long wars that would have impoverished the populations and created perilous dissension. In addition to these political reasons, however, Hadrian was inspired to travel out of sheer curiosity that was instilled in this extremely educated man who always sought to learn and was animated by the desire to visit places celebrated in history books as well as unknown regions; he was attracted by the possibility to expand his knowledge in every field of study. Thus, upon passing Sicily on a return journey to Italy, he could not resist the opportunity to climb Mt. Etna, to observe the volcano up close; similarly, he took advantage of his sojourn in Greece in order to study the Eleusian mysteries (he was eventually initiated into this cult), inspired by his interest in esoteric religious practices. Hadrian undertook two long journeys during his reign, each of which lasted several years: between 121 and 125 and between 128 and 133–134.

On his first voyage the emperor headed north, visiting Gaul, Germany and Britain, and going as far north as the border of Scotland, where he saw to the construction of the famous *Vallum*; upon his return through Gaul, he stopped at Nîmes, where he built a basilica in honor of Plotina, Trajan's wife, and from there traveled to Spain, staying in Tarragona: here he ordered the restoration of the Temple of Augustus, then proceeded toward Africa, crossing the Strait of Gibraltar, to arrive, finally, in the province of Syria, which was being threatened by the Parthians. From this moment Hadrian headed toward the East and Greece, although we do not always know the exact itinerary that he followed. He certainly crossed Asia Minor, where he encountered the young Antinous, and was determined to reach Asia by the beginning of the summer of AD 124. On his return journey, he spent several months in Greece, especially in Athens, where he was elected archon for the second time and served as judge in the festivities in honor of Dionysus; he stayed in Eleusis, where he was initiated into the cult, and also visited central Greece. In the summer of 125, he finally decided to return to Italy, stopping in Sicily, where he made an excursion to the summit of Mt. Etna. The emperor's second great journey outside of Italy was even longer, settling again in Greece in 128, following a brief sojourn in Africa. Once again he stayed in Eleusis and Athens, where he commissioned a widespread program of restoration that witnessed the completion of the colossal temple of Olympieion Zeus, which had stood unfinished for centuries. The Athenians, who celebrated by erecting twelve honorary statues, one for each tribe, founded a thirteenth tribe in his honor, giving it his name. The interest that moved the emperor, bringing him to many sites in Greece that were connected to history and myth (Argos, Sparta, Thespie), inspired him to dedicate particular attention to the cities he encountered, restoring the public buildings and improving their appearance; hence, the local populations proclaimed him to be the liberator. Subsequently, Hadrian traveled to Asia Minor, visiting, among many other cities, Ephesos, Tralles and Antioch, where he had been posted as procurator prior to succeeding Trajan; he reached Palmyra and finally Judea, where he founded the colony Aelia Capitolina (Jerusalem). In the summer of 130, the Imperial court went to Egypt and, from Alexandria, where Hadrian remained for some time, followed the course of the Nile, allowing the emperor to admire the principal cities along the way. The trip was blemished, however, by the tragic death of the young Antinous in the waters of the Nile. In honor of his companion, Hadrian founded the city of Antinoopolis, and then the voyage continued through other portions of Egypt until the beginning of 131, when the emperor decided to return to Athens. At the end of 133 or the early part of 134, Hadrian made his definitive return to Rome by way of Pannonia.

Map of Egypt with
the principal cities
visited by Hadrian.

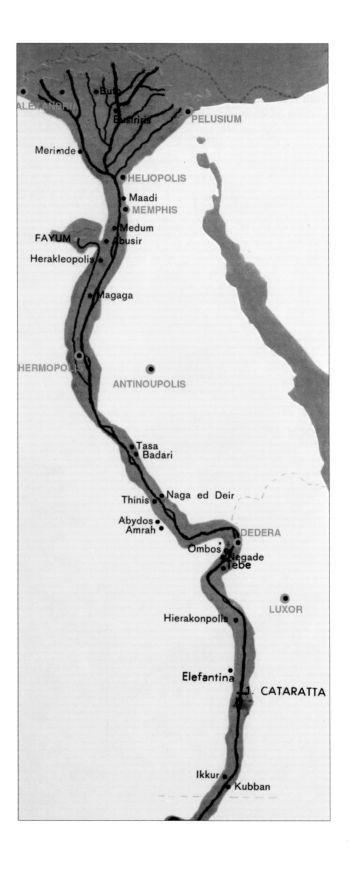

sions) not only because he unquestionably adored the culture, but for political motives as well: the eastern states that had been forced into the Roman Empire, apart from a variety of local dialects, spoke Greek. Recognition of the work he commissioned in the provinces came in the form of a tribute by the writer Helius Aristides, of Asian origin, who, upon the death of the emperor, made a public eulogy in Rome wherein he admired the form of government, the sense of justice, and the guarantee of security and order in the civic life in all cities. Furthermore, he emphasized the fact that Hadrian treated each of the regions of the Empire differently, according to their unique needs and traditions, in order to give everyone the feeling that they were part of a collective nation, i.e., a singular component in a large system in which many races co-existed. Such a positive image, that mirrors Hadrian's illuminated program, was nevertheless destined to be short-lived, in that it met considerable opposition from the ruling class of Rome, who felt that their privileges had been threatened through the introduction of new men. On the other hand, the Greek-speaking cities, which Hadrian favored and nurtured, constituted a minority in comparison with the masses of people who populated the Empire, living in vast territories in a semi-nomadic state. These populations refused integration with civilization and represented a continuous threats in terms of security along the borders and the stability of order.

The island of Philae and Hadrian's Gate in a 19th-century drawing.

Philae, the interior
Hadrian's Gate, during
one of the rare moments
of sun.
The relief shows the Nile
Grotto, with the God
of the Flood in the act
of making the waters rise,
while the Goddess Hathor
presents an offering in the
Garden of Osiris (or the
sacred lake), in an attempt
to resurrect Osiris
in the presence of Isis.
The God is represented
in the form of a bird
with a human head
whose features were later
rendered unrecognizable
through intentional
chiselling.

Antinous

The ancient sources only furnish scanty information about the handsome youth who became Hadrian's companion; the tales are generally related to the events leading up to his dramatic demise. He was born in Bithynium/Claudiopolis, a city of Bithynia in Asia Minor, probably around AD 110, and appears to have met the emperor during the course of Hadrian's first long voyage in the East, between 123 and 125. This would explain the great interest that Hadrian demonstrated toward this region, which was certainly not among the most important areas of the Empire at the time, and which, apart from being the object of special concessions, passed from the rank of Senatorial province to that of Imperial province. We know from a letter written by Hadrian that in AD 130 Antinous followed the Imperial court; writing to his brother-in-law, Julius Servianus after his departure from Alexandria, one of the first stops on his journey to Egypt, the emperor lamented the city's ungratefulness toward him, expressed through

a series of malicious rumors against his favorites, Antinous and Verus (Lucius Ceionius Commodus Verus, later adopted with the name of Lucius Helius Caesar), who had been in his company. The expedition was traveling up the Nile when in Besa, on the right bank of the river, in front of the city of Hermopolis, the young Bithynian met his death under mysterious circumstances. The official version reported by Spartianus in *Vita Hadriani* mentions a fatal fall into the river, but at the time, the facts of the event led to rumors of a suspected suicide (or even a homicide), possibly in order to save the emperor's life through a tremendous sacrifice. What is certain is that Hadrian demonstrated exasperating pain in light of this tragic death and manifested his affection for the youth through his immediate divinization—an honor reserved exclusively for emperors or members of the Imperial family—and expected him to be honored among the divinities of the Pantheon. Hadrian erected many temples and even a city, Antinoopolis, not far from the place of the fatal episode, to his new god.

While we know nothing of Antinous's character, nor of his qualities apart from his celebrated beauty, we are able to reconstruct the fundamental elements of his physical being through an examination of a great number of images that have come down to us in the form of effigies on coinage, statues and relief sculpture, that are obviously idealized, but present some common traits that can be reduced to an original model. A melancholic fascination emerges, characterized by large eyes highlighted by arched eyebrows and a sharp contrast between the full forms of his facial features and the hairstyle consisting of thick wavy locks that frame his face to the top of his ears. The fullness of his cheeks and the absence of any hint of facial hair indicate the extreme youth of this lad. Among the most beautiful portraits are an unprovenienced bronze now in the Archaeological Museum in Florence, the gemma Marlborough and a marble bust from Hadrian's Villa, discovered in the 18th century in the area of the Pantanello, now in the Hermitage.

Bronze portrait of Antinous.
Florence, Archaeological
Museum.

Portrait of Antinous.
St. Petersburg, Hermitage.

Gemma Marlborough, copy.
Paris, private collection.

The Architectural Plan of the Villa

Hadrian's Villa occupies a low plain composed of tufa stone at the foot of Monti Tiburtini, bordered by two streams, Acqua Ferrata to the east and Risicoli or Roccabruna to the west, which unite into a single channel that feeds into the Aniene river, not far from Ponte Lucano, where the via Tiburtina crosses the river as it climbs toward Tivoli (Tibur). The surface area, which we do not know the precise extent of, was certainly greater than the archaeological area seen today and must have spread over at least 120 hectares; only a portion of the land was built upon, while the remainder was left in a more or less natural state. In order to supervise the construction of this grandiose complex, Hadrian decided to move his official residence outside the capital, choosing an untouched area that had a rich water supply, both key prerequisites; the villa, well connected and very close to Rome (17 Roman miles from Porta Esquilina, corresponding to 28 kilometers), could also be approached by means of the Aniene river, navigable at the time. This area hosted numerous quarries from which the Romans extracted prime building material—travertine (used in the lower portions of the villa's structures), lime from limestone, pozzolana (a type of sand) and tufa—and was also the passageway for the four principal aqueducts that led to Rome and furnished the city with large volumes of water, indispensable for the many baths and fountains. In the

following pages
Plan of Hadrian's Villa
with the most commonly
used names of the
buildings.

1. Greek Theater
2. Gymnasium
3. Nympheum with the Temple of Venus
4. Tempe Terrace
5. Tempe Pavilion
6. Imperial Triclinium
7. Hospitalia
8. Lower Terrace of the Libraries
9. Upper Terrace of the Libraries
10. Latin Library
11. Greek Library
12. Courtyard of the Libraries
13. Cryptoporticus with Mosaic Vault
14. Imperial Palace
15. Gardens of the Palace
16. Exterior Peristyle
17. Piazza d'Oro
18. House South of the Piazza d'Oro
19. Gladiators' Arena
20. Stadium
21. Casa Colonica
22. Building with Doric Pillars
23. Guard Barracks
24. Baths with Heliocaminus
25. Maritime Theater
26. Terrace of the Maritime Theater
27. Philosophers' Chamber
28. Pecile
29. Hundred Chambers
30. Building with Three Exedras
31. Nympheum-Stadium
32. Building with Fish Pond
33. Quadriporticus
34. Small Baths
35. Area between Grand and Small Baths
36. Cryptoporticus near the Large Baths
37. Large Baths
38. Vestibile
39. Pavilion of the Praetorium
40. Eastern Substructures of the Canopus
41. Western Substructures of the Canopus
42. Canopus
43. Roccabruna
44. Esplanade of the Roccabruna
45. Esplanade of the Accademia
46. Accademia
47. Odeon

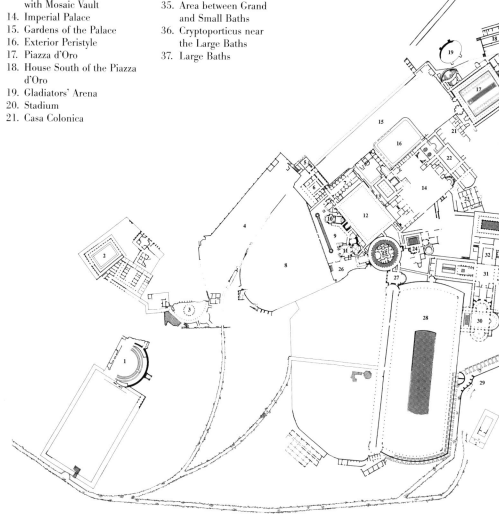

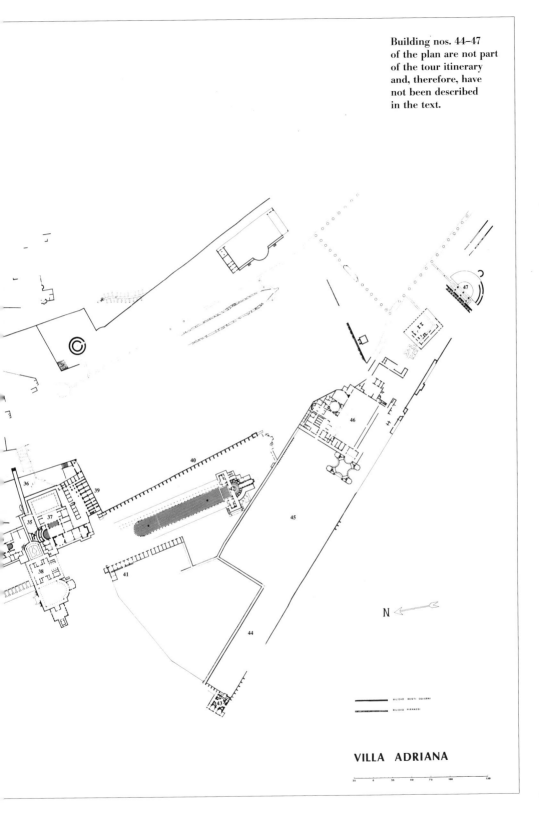

Building nos. 44–47
of the plan are not part
of the tour itinerary
and, therefore, have
not been described
in the text.

N

RILIEVO RESTI ODIERNI

RILIEVO PIRANESI

VILLA ADRIANA

Arpocrates. Rome, Capitoline Museum.

Faun in antique red marble. Rome, Capitoline Museum.

vicinity, at Acque Albule, there were several curative sulfur springs, the Bagni di Tivoli, that are still in use today and were well known by the emperor.

The archaeological area that can be visited today, about 40 hectares, contains an impressive and well preserved group of buildings whose plans and functions varied considerably from pavilions to gardens and nympheums, that were arranged along multiple and unaligned axes, that give the appearance of haphazard construction, but actually respond to the natural lay of the land. The peculiarity of the general plan and the obtrusive presence of spherical domes, cross domes and segment domes that are alternated with sloped roofs, a relentless combination of curves and straight lines that is also evident in the plans of the buildings, has led scholars to the conclusion that Hadrian, himself, was responsible for the design of his residence. That Hadrian dabbled in architecture is known through tales passed down to us by Cassius Dion who recalled the emperor's disputes with Apollodorus of Damascus who offered critical judgments toward the works of the future emperor; but even another writer, Aurelius Victor, confirms his activities as architect, specifying that Hadrian dedicated himself to this art during his sojourns at the villa in Tivoli. We can state without a doubt, based upon the testimony offered by architectural works that are still preserved from the Hadrianic era, such as the Pantheon or the Mausoleum of Castel Sant'Angelo, that the emperor was a truly gifted architect who worked with highly refined techniques, which he probably learned, in part, from Apollodorus, to whom modern scholars attribute the planning of the Pantheon, and from Decrianus, the architect who Hadrian entrusted with the responsibility to transfer the Colossus of Nero, in order to construct the temple of Venus and Rome.

Set on the property of an existing Republican villa, some of whose structures were incorporated into the area of the "Imperial Palace," Hadrian's residence should be considered to be the result of a single campaign of planning, based upon recently conducted studies, especially those which have focused on the subterranean passages and the water and sewage systems. Because we are dealing with such a monumental project, it should not be surprising that the individual structures were not erected simultaneously. This is indicated by the maker's marks on many bricks found in the walls, which

Temple of Venus, detail
of the upper portion
(*anastilosis*).

were manufactured at different times during this epoch and
suggest that the buildings of this massive undertaking were
constructed roughly from north to south. The fact that portions of buildings were very obviously modified (archaeologists and architectural historians have recognized features
such as closed or reconfigured apertures and improvised
additions to some structures) should not be viewed as a
consequence of later remodeling; rather, it is highly likely

Model of Hadrian's Villa,
created by the architect
I. Gismondi in 1956
for the archaeological
area of Hadrian's Villa.

Hadrian's Villa, pavilion
in the model, detail with
the Torre di Roccabruna.

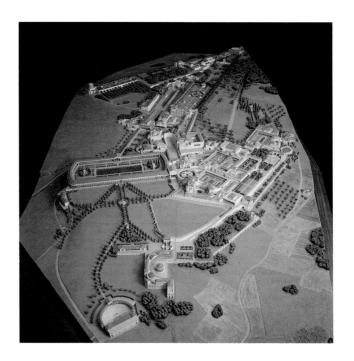

that the changes are the result of direct interventions on
the part of the emperor during the periods in which he
resided at the villa and was able to supervise the building
activities.

Observing the general plan of the complex, it appears evident that the buildings, approximately thirty of them,

were placed according to three divergent axes, only one of which, the one that ran along the area developed around the Republican villa, followed traditional conceptions of architectural style. The other two axes diverge decidedly from this first nucleus and follow completely different schemes, which were dictated in part by nature of the topography, but also adapted to and complemented the new kinds of designs chosen for the imposing buildings. However, scholars have not always been successful in determining the function of some buildings: the identification of the three bath complexes is certain and was necessary considering the great number of people who lived in and visited the villa, from the Imperial court and guests to the numerous servants who worked on the premises; the Pecile served as a gymnastic facility. The double *ambulacrum* to the north is a *porticus miliaria*, or measured porticus and by walking seven times around the massive wall, one covered the distance of two Roman miles: a rigorous walk after lunch was advised for good health. The area occupied by the Imperial Palace and the Building with a Fish Pond (or Winter Palace, based on the fact that one of the floors was furnished with a heating system) was closely connected to the garden and nympheum of the so-called Stadium and Building with Three Exedras, a series of spaces that formed a monumental entryway. All of these structures are considered to be part of the official residence of the emperor and his court. Another cluster of buildings includes the Hundred Chambers or Praetorium, where the rooms, arranged on several stories that were accessible by means of wooden walkways, are located in the massive substructures of the Pecile complex and, instead, were used by servants, as well as for the storage of goods. The presence of common latrines confirms the hypothesis that this area served as housing for the villa's personnel. These spaces were directly connected by a system of underground pas-

Marble cup with supports in the form of griffins' paws, from the Piazza d'Oro.

Marble vase with floral decoration in relief, from the Canopus.

sageways that served during the phase of construction to facilitate the transport of building materials and were subsequently used by the servants who ran the villa, so that they would not interfere with the life of the court.

The residential complex was embellished by a conspicuous display of sculpture. So precious were the works that a long period of frenetic and systematic treasure hunting began during the Renaissance. The stripping of marble, which already began during the Middle Ages for various building projects, led to the dispersion of so many decorative pieces of the villa, that nearly all of the major museums and collections in Rome and the rest of Italy, if not all of Europe, hold relics taken from Hadrian's Villa. Without counting examples whose provenience is unknown, researchers are aware of at least five hundred examples of statuary that were unearthed through the centuries in the various portions of the villa. Many works of sculpture were recovered from secondary deposits, such as the group rediscovered in the Pantanello swamp by Gavin Hamilton in the 18th century, where pieces of art had been piled at an unknown period of time, after they had been removed from the villa.

Based upon an examination of the sculpture preserved to this day, it is evident that the design of the spaces and the environments of the villa and the choice of the individual decorative programs were the result of meticulous planning: apart from the information gathered from written sources that indicate Hadrian's direct involvement in the determination of the villa's furnishings, the presence of certain kinds of statues and figural themes in some buildings and not others and the preference for rare marble and stone, chosen for their colors that closely reflect the nature of the subject being represented also suggests the emperor's tastes.

Head of a deer.
Vatican City,
Vatican Museums.

Peacock.
Vatican City,
Vatican Museums.

Plan of Hadrian's Villa that indicates the network of subterranean passageways that linked the various zones of the complex and the locations where works constituting the decorative program were recovered (E. Salza Prina Ricotti).

In addition to the articulated sequence of buildings and pavilions, which, as evinced by the judgment of ancient writers, must have given the impression of exceptional splendor, the villa was complemented by a series of gardens and open areas with fountains and nympheums that were the visual foci of certain spaces. Even though the upper portions of many buildings have been destroyed and we often walk along open spaces that were once occupied by closed structures, as with the case of the Imperial Palace or the Vestibule, and although we are not fully able to appreciate the system of gardens and other green spaces planned by Hadrian, their importance in the context of the villa is obvious. The peristyles and ample gardens were embellished by fountains, statues and other kinds of decorative features. The landscape that surrounded and was integrated into the "palace" was characterized by a succession of pavilions, towers, nympheums, architectural backdrops and residential buildings, that presented an insistent repetition of suggestive and unexpected visual perspectives, often emphasized by water features. The search for equilibrium between architectural features, in a strict sense, and nature, that is only apparently spontaneous, unquestionably constitutes one of the principal aspects at the base of the general design of the villa. The accomplishment of this grand architectural project caused, in effect,

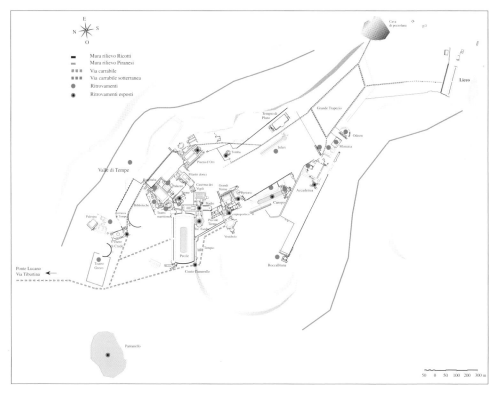

the manipulation of the original morphology of the plain upon which the residence was located, in some instances with the removal of large mounds of earth in order to accommodate valley-like features, as with the Canopus, and in other cases with the creation of artificial earth works that would host the new buildings, such as with the Pecile, in whose western flank the Hundred Chambers was situated.

There must have been secluded areas, surrounded by nature and in elevated positions. It seems probable that the overlying pavilion, cooled and shaded by the woods, and mentioned by Spartanius as the Tempe, was originally faced with precious marble, indicating its inclusion among the Imperial residence, and planned to serve as a point from which the beautiful panorama could be observed. Similarly, the Torre di Roccabruna, which was considerably taller than it is at present judging from the massive walls, also functioned as a viewing station that overlooked the graceful Roman countryside.

In recent decades, research conducted on the terrain upon which Hadrian's Villa is set has allowed scholars to better comprehend the organization of the "green areas" of the villa, through the careful study and documentation of each zone of the excavations, particularly in the gardens of the Piazza d'Oro, the Nympheum-Stadium, the so-called Throne Room (in the Building with Doric Pillars) and the Canopus. However, it has not been possible, based on the current body of evidence, to determine the specific types of vegetation that flourished in the villa's gardens. The arrangement of tall deciduous and evergreen trees (oaks, holm-oaks, ashes, cypresses and umbrella pines) that are seen today, by now part of a historicized context, was installed by Count Giuseppe Fede, the proprietor of a large part of the villa in the 18th century. This natural patrimony is now inseparable from the context of the ancient structures, together with about four thousand olive trees that have been cultivated since the Middle Ages for the production of oil. Among the trees is a massive cypress between the Nympheum and the Temple of Venus, in whose trunk (4.3 meters in diameter) an elm tree has grown, and, not far away, the only example of a *taxus baccata*, with its characteristic umbrella form; in the vicinity of the Canopus, on the border of the Roccabruna olive orchard, is the so-called "Albero Bello," an olive tree whose three-stemmed trunk measures more than five meters in diameter.

The Components of the Villa

The villa constructed by Hadrian near Tivoli must have been very impressive to the ancient Romans, if the biographer Helius Spartianus wrote of it with such great admira-

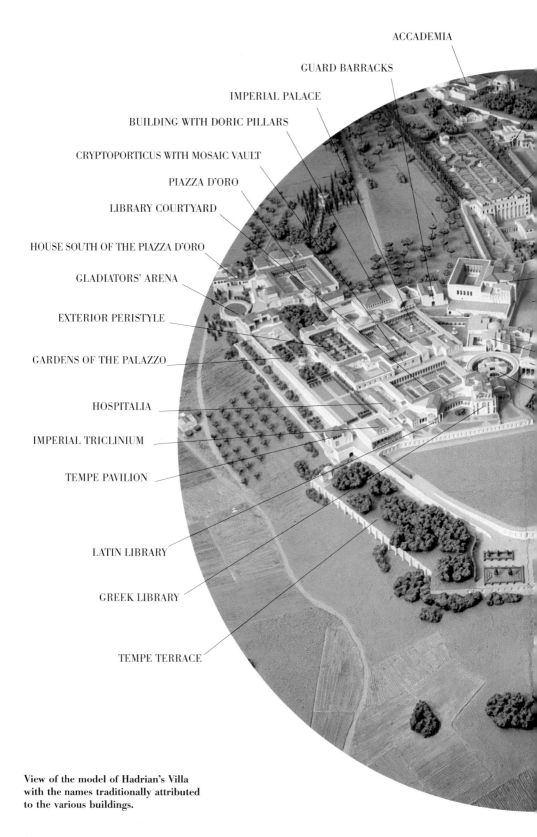

ACCADEMIA

GUARD BARRACKS

IMPERIAL PALACE

BUILDING WITH DORIC PILLARS

CRYPTOPORTICUS WITH MOSAIC VAULT

PIAZZA D'ORO

LIBRARY COURTYARD

HOUSE SOUTH OF THE PIAZZA D'ORO

GLADIATORS' ARENA

EXTERIOR PERISTYLE

GARDENS OF THE PALAZZO

HOSPITALIA

IMPERIAL TRICLINIUM

TEMPE PAVILION

LATIN LIBRARY

GREEK LIBRARY

TEMPE TERRACE

View of the model of Hadrian's Villa with the names traditionally attributed to the various buildings.

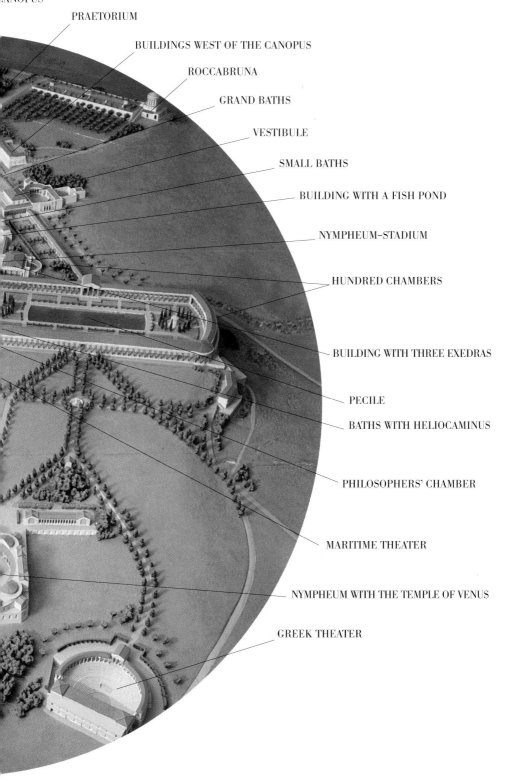

CANOPUS

PRAETORIUM

BUILDINGS WEST OF THE CANOPUS

ROCCABRUNA

GRAND BATHS

VESTIBULE

SMALL BATHS

BUILDING WITH A FISH POND

NYMPHEUM–STADIUM

HUNDRED CHAMBERS

BUILDING WITH THREE EXEDRAS

PECILE

BATHS WITH HELIOCAMINUS

PHILOSOPHERS' CHAMBER

MARITIME THEATER

NYMPHEUM WITH THE TEMPLE OF VENUS

GREEK THEATER

tion, specifying the peculiar fact that within the complex, the individual structures had assumed the names of some of the most celebrated locations in the provinces (Lyceum, Accademia, Pritaneo, Canopus, Pecile, Tempe) and even recalled the *Inferi* (gods of the underworld). Thus, for example, the latter were recognized in the area adjacent to the Piazza d'Oro, characterized by a prevalence of green space and crossed by galleries and subterranean paths, while the Tempe has been associated with the wooded valley below the lower terrace of the Libraries that faces the Acqua Ferrata stream. The Pecile has been identified as the massive porticoed courtyard that overlies the Hundred Chambers, while the Canopus is the long basin of water with a Serlian feature that terminates in a large pavilion with a *triclinium*, situated beyond the Vestibule. In reality, the difficulty in associating features with the names provided by Spartianus lies in the fact that the various buildings are not exact reproductions of the celebrated places reported in the written sources. But, aside from the hypotheses and attempts to name the structures in the past, an argument that scholars have been grappling with since the Renaissance, when a scientific interest in Hadrian's Villa was born, we must highlight the notion of universality in the villa. In a sense, the villa mirrors Hadrian's conception of the Empire, seen as a plurality of cultures, each with its own unique identity, that had been amalgamated into a common nation, represented by the Greco-Roman world. In Hadrian's Villa this becomes particularly evident in the case of the Canopus, possibly the only feature that has been identified with certainty on the basis of the ancient sources: its form unquestionably evokes a sense of the canal that united Alexandria and the city of Canopus, on the Nile delta, famous for the temple of Serapis. Yet from an architectural perspective, this complex is rather far removed from the world of Egypt and is actually more characteristic of the Greco-Roman tradition of style, despite the presence of certain solutions and peculiar elements. The presence of maker's marks stamped on a large proportion of bricks in the various components of the Canopus, refutes the common belief, derived from a reference in Spartianus text, that the emperor desired to reproduce the places that impressed him the most on his many voyages, since this feature was constructed prior to Hadrian's first journey to Egypt. The fact that not even the Canopus was a proper reconstruction of a celebrated monument should not be surprising; the names attributed by the ancient sources to the various architectural components of the villa should be interpreted as semi-invented references. We know, in fact, that the Romans, already by the Republican period, used to apply the names of famous locations to particular areas in their pleasure villas: for example, Cicero reports that he constructed an Accademia and a Lyceum on his estate in Tusculum; in some gardens artificial canals were installed that loosely imitated the Nile and contained references to Egypt, as well as the *Euripus*, the narrow passage of the sea that separates Euboea and Attica. Similarly, Augustus tells us that his home on the Palatine Hill contained a space that he called Syracuse, after the city in which Dionysius the Elder erected his palace, famous for being a building isolated by a canal.

The Phases of Construction

Set into the walls of many buildings, approximately half of those studied, were bricks bearing impressed stamps or maker's marks that indicate consular dates or the names of the two consuls who held office at the moment of production; since the fabrication of lots of bricks was performed on an annual basis, it has been possible to reconstruct a precise chronological framework, that allows scholars to date single examples. Based upon their presence in the walls of Hadrian's Villa, H. Bloch hypothesized a sequence of construction that involved the raising of buildings in three distinct phases: from 118 to 125, from 125 to 133/134 and from 133/134 to 138 AD. However, recent studies propose just two phases, wherein the first phase witnessed the greatest amount of building activity which appears to have terminated by AD 125, upon Hadrian's return from his first long journey in Greece and the East. In fact,

Example of a Republican period floor.

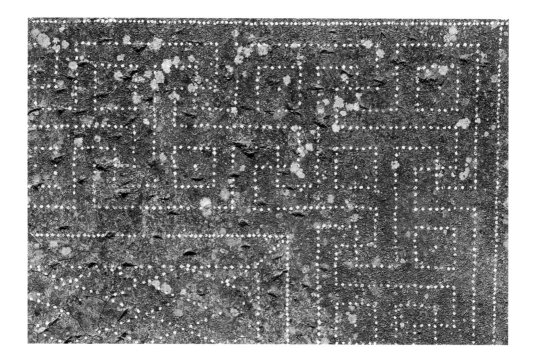

Pilaster strip capitals.

at the end of the summer of that year the emperor wrote to the inhabitants of Delphi from his villa in Tivoli. On the one hand, this confirms that the villa had been designated as his official residence; on the other hand, it seems unlikely that Hadrian would have chosen to reside on an estate that still required tremendous construction efforts. And the villa would have been largely unfinished, if we abide to the three-phase theory.

One strong piece of evidence derives from the brick stamps, most of which date to the years 123 and 124; the fact that the majority of the buildings that contained bricks bearing maker's marks from this period (even when they co-occurred with later brick stamps) attests to a peak in building activity coinciding with the first phase. There are very few brick stamps dated to earlier periods, all of which are present in structures that are known to have been among the first constructed, based upon their position within the complex. These are dated to AD 117 in the case of the Maritime Theater and the Philosophers' Chamber, and pre-123 in the case of the Baths with Heliocaminus as well as all buildings erected around the pre-existing Republican villa. The second phase, corresponding to brick stamps dating from 126 and later, involved the completion of a number of buildings, including the Building with a Fish Pond and the Piazza d'Oro, both of which also contain maker's marks from the years 123 and 124.

Architectural Decoration

The abandonment of the villa and the successive period in which the structures were stripped of their architectural members and other precious materials for reuse in Medieval and later buildings, together with the robbing of art and other decorative features, led in some instances to the complete loss of embellishments and we are often faced with architectural skeletons. Despite the impressive and grandiose walls, very little remains of the facings of vaults, walls and floors; hence, scholars are unable to present an accurate image of the villa's splendor during the age of Hadrian. Nevertheless, from the fragments that are still *in situ* and archaeological finds from the interior areas of the villa, we know that the decorative schemes used to complement the architecture of this grand complex were very rich and sumptuous.

The villa was constructed almost entirely in the *opus mixtum* technique, whereby the walls consisted of a cement core into which cut stones (wedge-shaped tufa blocks) were inserted to create the facing; the stones were arranged in a reticulate fashion that were bordered by horizontal rows of brick. The walls were then covered by a layer of plaster and were often embellished with frescoes, marble molding or

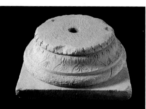

decorative stucco work. A particularly refined area is the stuccoed vault in one of the recently restored spaces in the Nympheum with the Temple of Venus that consists of geometric partitions emphasized with colors and isolated decorative motifs (flowers, peltae, ovules), as well as notable examples from the Grand Baths, whose style is more cursive. The walls and floors of the most important areas of the villa saw the use of precious and often rare marble, that was quarried from many corners of the Empire and assembled according to refined inlay techniques with elegant chromatic effects. At times the patterns were completed through the use of other kinds of material, such as glass paste and ivory. Especially significant are a fragmentary column capital and friezes consisting of colored marble inlays set into a slate background, as well as several fragments representing the face of a human subject and the wavy locks of hair of another, which indicate the original presence of figured friezes. Of slightly poorer quality are

mosaic floors. In only rare instances did archaeologists recover particularly important mosaics. These include scenes depicting a skirmish between centaurs and beasts, now in the Berlin Museum, theatrical masks, currently in the Vatican Museums, and doves, in the Capitoline Museum, all of which were assembled in the *vermiculatum* technique, which some scholars believe were actually Hellenistic works that were imported to the villa at Tivoli. Another very special work that demonstrates the impressive capabilities of mosaicists in the 2nd century AD is the polychrome mosaic with geometric decorations from one of the apsidal spaces on the side of the Vestibule in the Piazza d'Oro, where very small *tesserae* of a wide range of color were combined to create a weft that recalls the woven pattern of a mat or a carpet. In other portions of the complex, for example in the Hospitalia, the chromatic effect was underscored by the alternation of black and white sections, using rather large *tesserae*, which nevertheless

Detail of the vault in an area of the Nympheum with the Temple of Venus bearing decoration.

resulted in a marvelous decorative effect. Each of the spaces present geometric-floral motifs that are quite different from one to the next, in a manner that brings the central space to the forefront: naturally, this space bore the richest decoration and by comparison made the floors of the secondary spaces seem far less elaborate, since

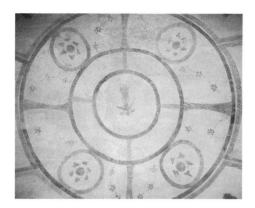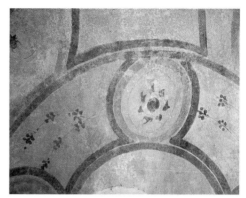

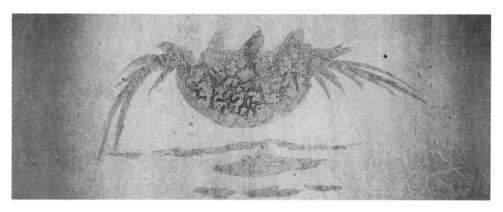

Fresco decoration from the vaults in the western substructures of the Canopus. The pictures, datable to the late 2nd–early 3rd century BC, demonstrate that the villa was occupied, at least through the Severan Dynasty, further confirmed by the imperial family portraits which have been found in the buildings.

these were destined to be less visible to prestigious guests. In addition to the rich program of wall facings, there is a notable group of architectural elements consisting of fragments of relief sculpture, trabeation, columns, column strips, column bases and capitals that are all characterized by sumptuous decoration, both ornamental and figured. These features are also of very high quality, and the typology and style of the architectural members confirms the splendor of the furnishings located throughout the noble buildings of the villa.

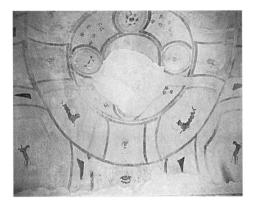

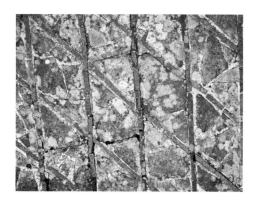

Fragment of wall
decoration in *opus sectile*
with polychrome marble
inlays on a base of slate.

Fragment of a pilaster
strip capital in *opus sectile*
with polychrome marble
inlays on a base of slate.

Examples of an *opus
sectile* floor.

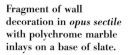

Examples of white
and black mosaic flooring.

Examples of a polychrome mosaic.

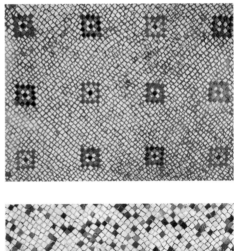

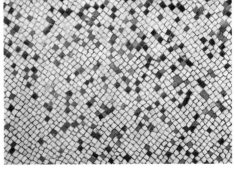

The Mosaic with Doves

This mosaic scene from an area of the Accademia was the central decorative element of the floor. Its refined technique saw the use of very small *tesserae* (*vermiculatum*) presenting the illusion that the image was painted. This was a close copy of a motif borrowed from a well known work by the artist Sosos. This painter, active in Pergamon (Asia Minor) in the 2nd century BC, supposedly created, as Pliny recalls, an "unswept floor" (*asarotos oikos*), that represented the immediate aftermath of a banquet; thus, the floor appeared to be "littered" with the remains of the feast. Among the many themes presented in the original works, whose compositional context is often unknown to modern researchers, is one that recurred throughout antiquity, namely doves drinking from a golden basin, a motif that is also noted in Pompeian mosaics, such as the example in the House of the Faun. In the 18th and 19th centuries, this motif was copied in mosaic, on tapestries and was ultimately adapted to suit a variety of craft goods manufactured during this period, all of which served different functions, were of various dimensions and were produced in different techniques: micro-mosaics, incisions on hard stone, paintings, etc.

The mosaic
with doves.
Rome, Capitoline
Museum.

Fragment of the
exterior border
of the mosaic
with doves.
Paris, Bibliothèque
Nationale.

The Rediscovery of the Villa

Centaur in gray marble.
Rome, Capitoline
Museum.

The true rediscovery of Hadrian's Villa, which had been frequented by artists during the Medieval period (we know of a drawing of the Greek Library by Francesco di Giorgio Martini) and other Humanists, including Flavio Biondo, occurred in the middle of the 16th century with the excavations conducted by Pirro Ligorio, when for the first time the complex was identified as the residence of the emperor Hadrian. Ligorio was the same architect that Cardinal Ippolito II d'Este commissioned to design his villa in Tivoli. This first widespread campaign of exploration, which brought important structures to light, including a number of fountains and nympheums that characterize the villa, inspiring Ligorio's plan of the Villa d'Este gardens, together with the quality and variety of marble statuary and the refined decorative programs, was the catalyst for the systematic robbery of antiquities undertaken by the proprietors of the land upon which the villa was set; the ruins were located on several pieces of private property. In the course of the 17th and 18th centuries, these treasure hunts were continued by the noble families who successively owned the land. The list of clandestine excavators includes the Jesuit priests who discovered a series of black marble statues, part of an Egyptian cycle, reportedly found in the area of the Canopus and now in the Vatican Museums. Notable finds were discovered in the excavations conducted by the Fede counts, who had the Casino Fede and Viale dei Cipressi built atop the ruins of the Nympheum and Temple of Venus. The road led to the Pecile, where Luigi Canina hacked a large rectangular portal into the principal wall of the courtyard, recognized by the absence of a *piattabanda* arch, in order to facilitate the passage of carriages toward the Canopus. Still in the 18th century, excavations by Cardinal Furietti saw the unearthing of two centaurs in gray marble, as well as the celebrated mosaic with doves from the Accademia building, all now in the Capitoline Museum. A number of high quality statues and pieces of relief sculpture were discovered in the second half of the century by the painter and art merchant Gavin Hamilton near the Pantanello swamp, a marginal area at the northern extremity of the villa, where marble fragments had been piled, possibly to be fired to produce lime, but were abandoned when the land became a marsh. It was only after the union of Italy that the site was protected, thanks to the interest of the superintendent Pietro Rosa, who managed to acquire most of the land comprised within the current archaeological area of Hadrian's Villa. Rosa initiated the scientific exploration of the site that was followed by Lanciani, Aurigemma, Vighi, and several foreign academies based in Rome.

Portrait of Lucius Verus. St. Petersburg, Hermitage.

The Buildings of Hadrian's Villa

Pecile

This monumental *quadriporticus*,
which surrounds a garden and a
large central pool, was intended to
represent the Pecile, the celebrated
Stoa Poikile in Athens, described in
the ancient sources, where the works
of the greatest Greek painters were
housed. The principal feature of the
northern side is a perfectly preserved
wall standing nine meters tall with a
monumental entrance at the center,
corresponding to a road that came
from the north. The sequence of
column bases arranged at regular
distances on both sides of the
wall indicates that a double portico
had been installed here. The roof
appears to have been a pitched
wooden structure, based upon a
series of large holes, visible in the
upper portion of the wall, into which
the heads of beams would have been
inserted. Today, plants in cylindrical
vases have been set on the plinths
of the peristyle in place of the
columns that supported the roof.
This section of the portico,
constructed prior to the remainder
of the complex, was intended for the
after-lunch stroll, as an inscription
discovered in this area during the
18th century recalls, which states
that the length of the portico itself
was 1450 feet, equivalent to 429
meters, equivalent to the distance
of an entire circuit around the wall.
The inscription continues, stating that
by following the course seven times,
one would have walked about two
Roman miles (ca. three kilometers).
Therefore, the length of the double
portico was calculated according
to the rules of a healthy walk
(*ambulatio*), determined by doctors,
as mentioned in the sources.
During the second phase of the
villa's construction the short ends
were added to the portico. These

slightly curved porticos close off the garden area at the center of which a large rectangular pool (approximately 100×25 meters) was installed. Unlike the current situation, where our vision is often misguided toward the inner region of the villa and beyond the perimeter of the Pecile, allowing magnificent views of the countryside, this garden was not considered with the idea of the surrounding panorama in mind. The tall walls that enclosed the columned portico would have impeded views of the landscape and served to "isolate" the park around the mirror of water, providing a peaceful and relaxing atmosphere. From this area residents and visitors could proceed into the Philosophers' Chamber or the Maritime Theater, to one side, and the Building with Three Exedras, the Nympheum-Stadium and the Building with a Fish Pond, on the other side, by means of a staircase.

Didactic Museum

Inside a small building erected in the late 18th century near the northwestern corner of the Pecile is the Didactic Museum. This permanent exhibition, arranged on three floors and complemented by explanatory panels, photos and drawings, is intended to focus visitors' attention onto three important notions: the planning and construction of Hadrian's Villa, the image of the villa in more recent history and the integration of the flora and fauna that create the "landscape."
In order to permit a detailed analysis of this monumental complex's development, the galleries within the Museum contain collections of original works discovered throughout the villa as well as reproductions of artifacts that have been exported over the course of time. One area of the museum displays the kinds of marble employed for wall facing and flooring as well as the different kinds of bricks and tiles used according to the function of the various structures and illustrations of the building techniques used. A separate showcase is dedicated exclusively to the maker's marks stamped onto bricks that were found throughout the villa complex, which scholars have studied in order to identify the names of the manufacturers and establish a chronological framework that has permitted them to date the structures to a narrow time period.
The image of Hadrian's Villa maintained in the 18th and 19th centuries is illustrated by a collection of prints obtained from original copper etchings held by the Calcografia Nazionale, which occupy an entire room of the museum. There are plans and other visual records of the entire complex and single monuments, which include several obviously inventive interpretations of some edifices and structural elements. Of great interest is the large etching by Giovan Battista and Francesco Piranesi, published in 1781, a first attempt, based upon scientific evidence, to establish the "plan of the buildings in Hadrian's Villa" and still represents an important point of reference for the reconstruction of many of structures that are only partially or no longer visible today.
Finally, a portion of the museum calls attention to the natural setting and landscape of Hadrian's Villa, with a consideration of the evolution of the kind of plants and trees that probably existed, in light of evidence gathered from the ancient written sources on the Romans' knowledge of *ars topiaria* as well as from the archaeological record.
In the centuries following the abandonment of the villa, the original man-made landscape was overtaken by spontaneous vegetation and species related to agricultural production, well documented in the drawings and photographs of this section. And this relationship between nature and architecture was certainly important during the phase in which the villa was occupied, albeit on a different scale and with a different appearance. This can be understood in the amount of space granted to gardens and the significant role that water played, seen in the numerous ponds, pools and fountains on the estate, and in one of the detailed plans in this guide.

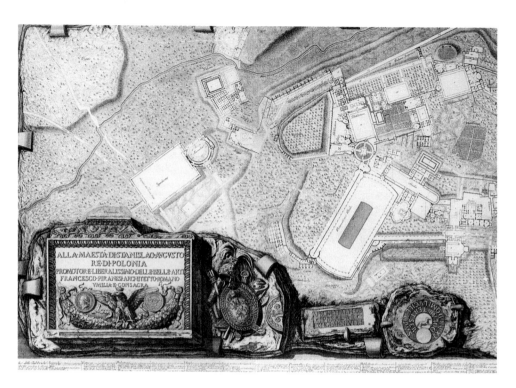

Plan of
Hadrian's Villa
by Giovan
Battista and
Francesco
Piranesi.

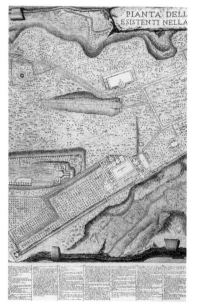

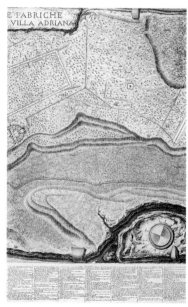

The Hundred Chambers

The creation of a level surface for the Pecile was possible through the construction of a massive system of substructures, the so-called Hundred Chambers, in order to compensate for the uneven terrain of the underlying valley, which reaches a depth of fifteen meters along the western side. As with most of the substructures of the villa, the supporting features are composed of a series of contiguous spaces, aligned on a maximum of four superimposed stories. The rooms, characterized by their identical dimensions, wooden floors and single entrance at the front, were accessible by means of a system of external walkways made of wood that were linked by a set of concrete stairs. The modest nature of the walls and floors, the great number of chambers, which inspired the name of the complex, and the fact that a paved road passing beneath the Vestibule by means of subterranean pathway provided direct access to the service spaces of the baths, has led scholars to speculate that this area was reserved for the housing of the humbler residents of the villa, the servants. That this area functioned as dwelling space is confirmed by the presence of communal latrines. Furthermore, it seems likely that the series of spaces set even with the road were utilized for the storage of goods and produce that served the quotidian needs of the villa, based upon the very easy access to the paved road and the presence, in some instances, of far lower ceilings compared to the chambers of the upper levels.

The Baths with Heliocaminus

View of
the circular
chamber.

Capital.

Aphrodite
of Doidalsas.
Rome, Museo
Nazionale
Romano in
Palazzo Massimo
alle Terme.

The oldest bath complex of the villa, constructed on a portion of the site of the former Republican villa and connected to the residential area by means of a hallway, owes its name to an impressive circular chamber that contains a *heliocaminus*, an environment heated by the rays of the sun (and later by portable stoves), utilized for sunbathers; such spaces are discussed in the ancient sources (e.g., Pliny, Epist., II.17).

Recently, a *sudatio* has also been identified, based upon the presence of furnace duct that heated the floors and walls of the area and provided the water vapor necessary for the sauna.
The chamber, roofed by a coffered dome with a central oculus, was furnished with large windows, that are no longer preserved, on the south-west side where the heated areas of this complex were situated;

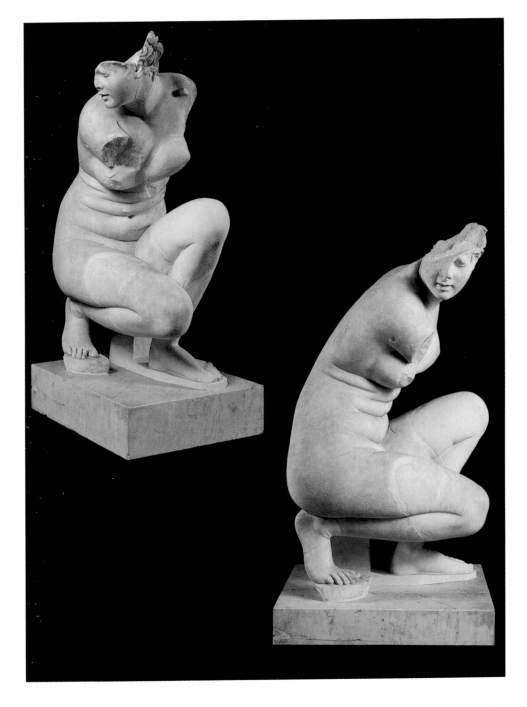

in fact all heated areas of the various baths in Hadrian's Villa faced this direction, an orientation prescribed by the architect Vitruvius. The south-west exposition exploited the hottest rays of the afternoon sun, when the Romans generally bathed. Flanking the *heliocaminus* is the *frigidarium*, an open rectangular space with a large pool surrounded by a colonnade; there was also a second, semicircular pool, which led to a heated chamber and finally, the *caldarium*.

This latter chamber, heavily damaged through the centuries, were two rectangular pools for hot baths set into niches. The original wall facing and flooring throughout the edifice consisted of sheets of marble, which has only been preserved in traces. This and the use of non-ornamental mosaic pavement in the service corridors and in the heated circular chamber, indicates that this bath complex formed part of the noble area of the villa.

Sudatio

The chamber for Turkish baths, the *laconicum* (a reference to Spartan customs) or *sudatio*, was a circular area containing benches along the walls, covered by a dome with a central *lumen* (oculus) that could be closed by a bronze plate. A chain was utilized to maneuver the plate in order to regulate the amount of steam in the chamber. The emission of water vapor into the air could have been achieved with portable stoves (as attested, for example, in Herculaneum), furnaces (as in the case of the chamber in the Baths with Heliocaminus), or by channeling natural vapors that were expelled from the earth (like at Baia). This chamber was also furnished with large windows that were arranged according to the path of the sun; the heat of the sunlight was intensified by glass panes, a discovery made in the 1st century AD. Because only small panes could be manufactured, large windows were sealed using a bronze or iron grid system that was inserted into the aperture. The glass was set into the metal frames with lead soldering.

The Philosophers' Chamber

This is a striking apsidal chamber, whose principal entrance was located to the north between a pair of columns *in antis*, that was named for the seven niches in the rear wall in which scholars believe statues of seven philosophers were displayed. The space was completely faced in marble, as the impressions of marble slabs in the plaster and holes in the wall serving as a support system for the sheets of precious stone attest. In addition, we have a short description by Pirro Ligorio which presents us with, at least, a partial vision of the original appearance of the chamber. The walls and floor were lined with porphyry and the ceiling was probably coffered.

Some researchers claim that this, in fact, was a library, interpreting the niches as shelving space for volumes of literature; however, the difficulty involved in accessing the niches, set above a tall baseboard, and extending upwards for 3 meters, along with the fact that they were only situated along a single wall of the chamber, would appear to refute this hypothesis. Considering the dimensions of the chamber, the use of porphyry, the adjoining Pecile to one side and Maritime Theater to the other, each accessible by means of two doorways, not to mention the analogy with the Auditorium (or Basilica) of the Domus Flavia on the Palatine Hill, known to have been used for official meetings, it seems more likely that the so-called Philosophers' Chamber was used to hold councils. The niches, therefore, would have borne a cycle of statuary, possibly of the Imperial family.

The Maritime Theater

Aerial view
of the building.

The is one of the best known monuments of Hadrian's Villa and has effectively become the symbol of the singularity and the innovation in the architectural design of the entire villa complex. The principal entrance of this edifice, consisting of a circular body preceded by a pronaos, is set to the north, leading onto the garden area of the Libraries that is connected to the lower Terrace. From the pronaos, which is only preserved in the form of column bases, one enters the atrium that is embellished on each side by a rectangular niche. An axial entrance leads to a circular portico, composed of Ionic columns that support a

vaulted roof, as demonstrated by the *anastilosis* of some columns and by the reconstruction of a portion of the vault, executed in the 1950s. The colonnade is reflected in the waters of a narrow moat that surrounds a circular island, upon which a building stood. Characterized by a continuous alternation of curves and lines, the circular structure should be considered to be a true *domus*, a sort of mini-villa within the Imperial residence. Currently, two cement bridges cross the moat, which were installed during the Late Antique

period; however, during Hadrian's reign the *domus* was approached by means of two portable wooden ramps that could be easily removed in order to give the impression that the island was inaccessible. On the base of the ring-shaped pool, that was lined with white marble, some of which is still preserved, are the perfectly legible grooves, in the marble itself, of the guides in which the bridges were slid into place. The

position of the bridges corresponded to the entrance, or *fauces*, situated outside the curvilinear atrium that was adorned with grooved Ionic columns, whose trabeation is characterized by a refined figured frieze carved in marble. The friezes bear marine themes, providing the modern name of this area. Beyond the atrium, is a portico with a peculiar shape: with convex inner walls and a small garden at the center which may have hosted a fountain. Adjacent to this, oriented axially, is a room flanked by two symmetrical spaces, with an open entryway on one side, in the form of an exedra delimited by Ionic columns, and a large window facing a rectangular niche in the rear wall of the circular portico. It is likely that the statue of a Faun carved in antique red marble that was found during the course of that 18th-century excavations in the Maritime Theater, and later acquired by the Vatican Museums (Gabinetto of the Maschere), was located in this niche or, in any event, in one of the other two niches in the building. Between these extremities was a private latrine, located in the spaces where the walls of the main chambers intersected with the circular perimeter wall of the island. On the east side are a pair of rooms with a cross-shaped plan which have been identified as *cubicola* (bedrooms), based upon the presence of an alcove overlooking the moat, where a bed would have been set. Instead, the western side was completely occupied by a small bath complex, evidently for private use: at the center was the *frigidarium* with a cold water basin that communicated, by means of a still-extant double stairway in cement, with the circular canal, that was apparently used as a *natatio*, or swimming pool, as well; just north of the *frigidarium* are the heated areas. From the external circular portico, a stairway led to the Courtyard of the Greek Library, while on the opposite side of the portico were a door and a corridor which faced a narrow space, probably a guard post. This connected the Maritime Theater with the Philosophers' Chamber. Opening onto the corridor, illuminated by a window, was a door leading to an uncovered area near the Baths with Heliocaminus, and a subterranean gallery, which contains an exceptional mosaic. Following the gallery, one could quickly enter the area of the Nympheum-Stadium. The edifice, whose general plan recalls that of the Pantheon (even their dimensions are roughly equal: 45 meters vs. the Pantheon's 43.5 meters), responds to the much sought after concept of isolation, already present in the notion of the Roman pleasure (*otium*) villa and its predecessors in the Greek world: the palace of Dionysius the Elder in Syracuse, consisted of a structure that was isolated by a canal, that, perhaps, Augustus sought to imitate in his urban residence on the Palatine Hill. We are told through the testimony of Suetonius (*Aug.* 72.2) that the first emperor's palace contained an area called "Syracuse" or "Laboratory," where he often sought refuge from the disturbances of daily life. Pliny the Younger, in his *Epistles* (II, 17.20–24), discusses his own place of refuge, a pavilion constructed on his property in the seaside town of Laurentum, that was designed like a true residence, almost a villa within his villa, that was far removed from the hustle

and bustle of the city. The sensation of finding oneself in a place where a person can retire and pursue his activities in perfect tranquillity can still be perceived by visitors to the Maritime Theater. Walking around this portion of the villa, views of the outside world are hindered by a tall wall around the portico that separates the island from the adjacent structures, rendering an isolated space that only opens onto the pronaos. At the rear, a fountain is situated along the principal axis and is visible at the end of a scenic sequence of columns, creating the illusion that the building's atrium is longer than it truly is. The internal space, although reduced and conditioned by the circular plan, was exploited in the best manner possible, allowing all of the spaces that the emperor required. And, in effect, the features of the construction repeat the typical scheme of the *domus*, with its atrium, courtyard, portico, *tablinum*, *cubicola*, bath complex and, even, latrine, all situated in this narrow space. The most interesting characteristic of this miniature villa is, perhaps, related to the functionality of the design that forces and adapts the required space in an aesthetic manner. Considering the artistic qualities attributed to Hadrian by the ancient sources and, in particular, his passion for architecture, and bearing the words of Pliny in mind, in which the writer explicitly claims to have designed the secret pavilion on his own estate in Laurentum, it is commonly maintained that the Maritime Theater represents the clearest evidence of the emperor's direct participation in the planning of his residence.

Library Courtyard

The Libraries

Contrary to what one might think about the commonly applied name of this area, this was not a courtyard related to the so-called Libraries, which is located on the opposite side. Rather, this was a pre-existing peristyle, reutilized in the Hadrianic era to serve as a passageway between the various buildings: Imperial Triclinium, Hospitalia, Imperial Palace, Baths with Heliocaminus, Maritime Theater and the Libraries. The presence of *opus incertum* walls in the portico, originally supported by columns with Corinthian capitals, demonstrates that this was part of the Republican villa. We do not fully understand the organization of the central zone, occupied today by an olive grove, since this area has never been excavated. However, scholars suspect that there was a series of gardens and, possibly, fountains, similar to the other peristyles of the villa. Even the rectangular nympheum situated to the north between the two Libraries was already part of the Republican complex, as the *opus incertum* building technique used for the interior walls would indicate. According to the transformations required by Hadrian, the walls of the nympheum were reinforced on the outside in order to install a cistern, still partially preserved above the vault, which increased the amount of water fed into the fountain, evidently in order to create new plays of water.

Set upon the artificial plain known as the upper Terrace, in the midst of a garden and bordered by a substantial wall embellished by niches and interrupted in the center by a staircase that linked the upper and lower floors, are a pair of buildings traditionally defined as the Greek Library and the Latin Library. The facades of the two structures, oriented toward the north, faced onto a garden with a long fountain that ran parallel to the perimeter wall of the upper Terrace. The buildings were joined by a portico. The Greek Library is arranged on three floors, of which the uppermost story, accessible from the ground floor by an external set of stairs that also led to the Maritime Theater, was furnished with a heating system. The service rooms and corridors, where the *praefurnia* (furnace) was located, were linked to the intermediate level, but did not communicate directly with the upper floor, according to a plan repeated in the Building with a Fish Pond. Today, visitors can only observe the lower floor, at the level of the garden, where despite the fact that the vault has collapsed onto the ground, it is possible to discern the two principal chambers, contiguous and arranged on the same north-south axis. These rooms are characterized by a series of rectangular niches along the walls and were originally paved in *opus sectile*. The remains of the vault in the front room reveal traces of mosaic facing. The organization of the Latin Library, on two stories, of which only the lower level is accessible, is similar to that of the Greek Library. This edifice also contains a pair of adjacent rooms set upon the same axis. The front chamber opens onto the garden with a fountain and also has rectangular niches along the walls; on the other hand, the apse at the rear of the second room is embellished by a platform for a group of statuary, visible from the exterior. Both spaces were faced with marble, both on the floor and on the walls. The two structures have been interpreted in several different ways: as libraries, due to the presence of the niches; as summer *triclinia*, due to their orientation toward the north where the garden lies; as towers that indicated the dwelling place of the emperor, which would adhere to descriptions provided by Vitruvius; or, more recently, as the monumental entrance to the palace. What is certain is that the presence of a heating system in the upper story of the so-called Greek Library, which assumes that this area was utilized during the winter months, indicates that at least this portion of the building served a residential function. The close proximity to the Maritime Theater, to which the building was directly connected, and the island-tower association, described in the written sources on the typology of pleasure villas, suggests that this area was used by the emperor.

The Hospitalia
and Imperial Triclinium

When Hadrian decided to erect his official residence on the site of the pre-existing Republican villa, he began to add new sections to the complex, transforming the extant spaces or incorporating them into elevations and substructures. The area of the so-called Hospitalia and Imperial Triclinium were clearly erected in this phase of building activity and were developed above the perimeter walls of the old villa's gardens. Despite the name Imperial Triclinium and the presence of beautiful, white and black mosaic floors with geometric and floral motifs that are among the best preserved in the entire villa, this area may not have been frequented by the Imperial court at all, as the complete absence of polychrome mosaics with figured panels and *opus sectile* flooring would suggest. On the contrary, this area may have been used by people of middle rank who were necessary to the emperor, probably

officials of the praetorian guard. The Hospitalia complex (or guest rooms), along one of the short ends of the Library Courtyard, consists of an ample corridor paved with white mosaic *tesserae* with black crosses, onto which a double series of *cubicola* open, each of which was furnished with three beds, whose positions are indicated by different designs on the mosaic floor, all geometric. The remainder of the paved space is decorated with floral elements that occur in a number of combinations. The walls were faced with painted plaster, which is only preserved in small areas. The central corridor terminates in an ample chamber with niches in the rear wall, whose construction technique (*opus quasi reticulatum*) indicates the reutilization of Republican period features. Another remnant of the earlier phase consists of the sides of the entrance to the *Cryptoporticus* with a mosaic on the interior surface of the vault, which in the Hadrianic phase remained accessible from the lateral corridor of the Hospitalia. The niches were incorporated into the rear wall of the principal space in the Hospitalia and plugged, with the exception of the central niche. The base of a statue was discovered *in situ* in front of the niche, suggesting the identification of this chamber as a cult shrine. An 'L' shaped trench in the adjacent area on the western side of the edifice has been demonstrated to have served as a communal latrine, while the principal latrine is located near the entrance, to the side of a cubiculum. Next to the latrine, but not in direct communication with it, is a stairway that was installed at a much later time which permitted access to the Library Courtyard. On the opposite side, another

**Flooring of one
of the chambers
of the Hospitalia.**

stairway led to the so-called Imperial Triclinium, centered upon a large room for the *coenatio* (dining room) that was paved with a white and black mosaic with rhombuses and was set between two corridors which gave access to many other chambers. The orientation of this chamber to the north and the presence of a portico with a terrace, added sometime after the original construction, suggests that this wing of the complex was utilized in the summer. Flanking the *triclinium* was a *cryptoporticus* with a white mosaic floor, that was illuminated by apertures in the ceiling and was connected by a secondary stairway to the Hospitalia, to one side, and, to the other side, of the garden leading to the Tempe Pavilion. The latter is an area situated below the pre-existing garden terraces that incorporated the Republican retention wall into its structure. The two edifices, however, were set below the level of the earthen foundation of the Republican villa, that was also used during the Hadrianic phase as a garden. In order to drain off rain water, a complex system of basins and channels was installed, which run close to the *cubicola*—taking advantage of the space between these and the Republican period retention wall as well as the spaces of the alcove—and continued below the floor of the *cryptoporticus* in the Triclinium. The Imperial Triclinium has also been proposed as the principal atrium of Hadrian's Villa, since the route of the Republican road passed from the north and proceeded beneath the small temple of Venus. However, as we have already mentioned, there was no way to enter from the lower terrace of the Libraries to the Triclinium terrace, whose perimeter wall appears not to have been considered important, if a portion of its eastern section was dismantled to construct the niched substructure of the Library Garden.

Terrace and Tempe Pavilion

Imperial Palace

Another area that Helius Spartianus mentions among the various structures in Hadrian's monumental residence in Tivoli is the Tempe, valley of the Tessaglia, associated with the artificial earthworks located beyond the Nympheum and temple of Venus, based upon the appearance of the cool and shady woods with oaks and other kinds of trees. Set upon the terracing, whose massive substructures are visible from the valley, is a three-story pavilion. The lower floor, termed "Stallone," consists of a large area with a central niche, encrusted with tartar or false stalactites, that connote the concept of a nympheum. At the beginning of the 19th century a fragmentary statue of Hercules was discovered in the niche. From this level an external ramp, imitated by the modern one, permitted one to reach the intermediate floor, adjacent to the Imperial Triclinium. Of the many rooms set on this floor, the chamber that faces the valley appears to have been the principal room, based upon its dimensions and position. The chamber was definitely covered, as the holes in the bare walls into which marble sheets would have been set suggest, and was originally paved, not with the *cocciopesto* surface seen today (laid during a 19th-century restoration), but with *opus sectile* like all the other rooms, including the latrines. The latter were located beneath the segment of the stairway that led to the upper floor, now almost completely razed to the ground. Visitors can still reach the upper gardens of the palace. The pavilion was used by the Imperial family and court to circulate between the Tempe Terrace and the residential zone of the palace, consenting external access from the Greek Theater to the Piazza d'Oro.

The Palace represents the primary nucleus of the Imperial residence, erected upon the site of the former Republican villa, portions of which were partially or completely incorporated into the Hadrianic structure; the Republican features are easily recognizable due to differences in construction techniques. Very well preserved, for example, is the *cryptoporticus* of the Republican edifice, whose vault was decorated by a mosaic composed of marble chips, glass paste, and seashells, which form prevalently geometric patterns set within concentric frames. In one extremity of the southern wing is a fountain set into a semicircular niche, contributing toward the sensation of freshness, particularly sought during the hot summer months. In the course of the Hadrianic phase, the subterranean gallery, with its unusual decoration that was originally highlighted by a fountain, was transformed into a service corridor, as the obliteration of the western wing attests, and subdivided into multiple spaces. Even the upper level was transformed through the demolition of the pre-existing structures in order to create a courtyard bordered by a portico. A stairway was the principal route between the Library Courtyard and the level of the Palace, articulated into several sectors, which alternated between courtyards and areas discovered to have been manicured gardens, surrounded by columns and pilasters. A vast garden area, known as the Upper Gardens was located along the eastern side, which served the same function in the Republican villa, but has not yet been studied in an appropriate manner. The unfortunate processes involved in the discovery of the different wings

of this massive complex witnessed
the robbing of precious furnishings,
architectural embellishments and
elements, and even compromised
the stability of certain structures,
rendering very difficult a comparison
between the plans reconstructed by
scholars and what actually remains
visible today. Recognizable in the
northern areas is a square space
that opens onto a courtyard with
pilasters overlying the Republican
cryptoporticus and is characterized
by a continuous series of small
rectangular and circular niches
in the rear wall. This has been
identified as a library: the niches in
the walls probably contained shelves
for the literary volumes. From one
of the two contiguous spaces, both of
which faced the porticoed courtyard,
one could proceed into the so-called
Triclinium of the Centaurs, an
apsidal chamber, oriented along
an east-west axis that was subdivided
into three naves by two rows
of columns. The particularly rich
and elaborate mosaic floor consisted
of figured scenes with a variety
of subjects: a group of centaurs
being assaulted by wild beasts,
today in the Berlin Museum, as well
as scenes with divinities and masks,
currently displayed in the Gabinetto
delle Maschere in the Vatican
Museums, where they have
been arbitrarily reassembled
with elements from other
portions of the villa.
In the central region, a white mosaic
floor with fragments of colored
marble is still visible. This was part
of the Republican villa's portico that
was reutilized during the Hadrianic
phase together with the *cubicola*
that face onto the eastern side
of the courtyard. From this space,
which today is simply a large open
area, one could proceed through

a doorway to a semicircular exedra
bordered by a row of columns,
beyond which was a courtyard
displaying the *opus spicatum*
technique. A large nympheum
was situated on the opposite side,
still partially buried, which mimics
the semicircular form of the exedra.
As evidence from the excavations
suggest, this area originally
contained a series of niches
with fountains bearing steps over
which water spilled into a basin
at the foot of the *cavea*.
On the far western end of the
Palace, near the Guard Barracks,
is the so-called Summer Triclinium,
a semicircular chamber that was
furnished with niches for statues and
fountains, which due to the presence
of a stone *stibadion* (semicircular
couch), no longer visible, suggests
that this served as a *coenatio*; only
the beginning of the vaulted roof
is preserved. This kind of structure,
characterized by plays of water
created by little waterfalls from
which water gushed into a channel
set to one side of the *triclinium*
couch, recalls the design of the
Serapeum, albeit in a strictly
simplified manner. Before the
chamber was a large garden.

Building with Doric Pillars

Near the Summer Triclinium and Republican exedras, built during the second phase of the villa's construction, was a structure that served as a passageway between various parts of the Palace, a sort of corridor between the areas aligned along the eastern axis and those located on the opposite side. From this edifice, one could reach the Summer Triclinium, the Building with a Fish Pond, the External Peristyle and the Piazza d'Oro. One entered a vast rectangular space with a portico with grooved pillars and Doric trabeation consisting of triglyphs and metopes (hence the name of the complex) by means of a corridor paved in mosaic consisting of small, differently colored rhombuses. The portico, partially reconstructed in the 1950s , was covered by a barrel vault and embellished by sheets of marble, both on the walls and on the floor. Much discussed is the question of the roofing system in the central area, which was paved with slabs of *bardiglio* marble arranged diagonally. Some researchers claim that the pillars supported a pitched, wooden roof, while others propose that the space was not covered at all and was thus a large courtyard rather than a true chamber. From the western side, one entered the principal area, flanked by a corridor and overlooking a second portico, this time with columns. Beyond the portico was an open space organized around a garden and terminating with an apse. At the center of the semicircular wall, ornate with niches, was a group of statuary of which only the bases remain. The archaeological investigations that demonstrated the existence of a garden area in this area have allowed scholars to reject the hypothesis that this was Hadrian's throne room.

View of the south-east corner of the *anastilosis*.

Piazza d'Oro

The Vestibule.

**Flooring
of the portico
in *opus sectile*.**

**Nympheum on
the south side,
on axis with
the Vestibule.**

The modern name is indicative of the very wealthy architectural and sculptural programs in the complex, which were systematically stripped from the structure through many fruitful excavation campaigns beginning in the 16th century led by "treasure hunters." From this site, numerous celebrated marble sculptures and architectural elements were discovered that are now part of the collections of many different foreign museums and private holdings. Despite all of the clandestine work, even by the end of the 18th century, there was still an impressive series of "columns in gray marble with Corinthian capitals" (Centini's excavations, 1783). These columns have been identified with the examples displayed in one gallery of the Vatican Museums, while several busts and portraits unearthed in the 19th century-excavations by Lanciani are currently housed in the Museo Nazionale Romano and at Hadrian's Villa in the Canopus Antiquarium. The importance and prestige of this wing of the villa, during Hadrian's lifetime, but even after his death, is emphasized by the discovery of many other Imperial portraits,

**Frieze with a
hunting scene.**

**Friezes with a
marine retinue.**

including those of Sabina,
Marcus Aurelius and Caracalla.
The edifice contains a large central
garden, lined longitudinally by
a long rectangular basin flanked by
a symmetrical series of flower beds
and basins and surrounded by a
grand portico with pillars and brick
semi-columns. The covered space was
subdivided into two naves by columns
in *cipollino* marble and green granite,
set in an alternating pattern, which
present double interaxial spaces with
respect to the pillars that face the
garden. Pillars with semi-columns,
also in brick, occur once again
along the rear wall of the portico,
embellished by small arches upon
pilaster strips. The masonry walls
were probably covered by painted
stucco or plaster. Along the long sides
were two corridors that ran parallel
with the portico and opened onto
a number of different spaces. One
approached the building by means
of a porticoed corridor, open on the

eastern side, with a flat ceiling, which
has been deduced from the presence
of holes along the upper portion
of the boundary wall of the portico
into which the wooden beams of
the ceiling were inserted. The tall
wall erected on this side separated
the entrance of this public zone
from the so-called Casa Colonica,
whose remains are visible behind the
northern portico of the Piazza d'Oro.
The Casa Colonica was a building
from the phase preceding Hadrian's
reign that is characterized by
a mosaic floor of modest quality,
suggesting that it was used
by the servants who ran the villa.
The entrance to the garden of the
Piazza d'Oro consists of a vestibule
with an octagonal form, upon
which alternately rectangular
and semicircular niches opened;
this was roofed by a segmented
dome with a large central oculus.
At one time this was framed between
two minor spaces with niches.

72

The western space, still partially preserved, bears a highly refined polychrome mosaic floor with rhombus motifs: the subtly different shades of color were obtained through the skillful application of the various tones and the use of very small *tesserae*.

On the opposite side of the garden, where the principal areas are situated, is an articulated sequence of space where very different architectural elements were daringly placed near each other and which contained scenographic effects of Hellenistic inspiration, that also included plays of water. At the center is a large chamber, among the most peculiar and discussed areas of the villa, that is characterized by a series of columns arranged in such a way as to form an octagonal plan whose sides were alternately concave and convex, inscribed within a square whose corners contain small apsidal nympheums. Six single latrines are

Portrait of
Marcus Aurelius.
Rome, Museo
Nazionale
Romano in
Palazzo Massimo
alle Terme.

Portrait of Vibia
Sabina.

located between some of the pillars.
According to some scholars, the
chamber was roofed by a bold dome;
however, other researchers maintain
that there was no roof at all. Still
other architectural historians
suggest that there was a pitched roof
consisting of a perishable material,
such as wood. The rear end was
occupied by a large semicircular
nympheum: the water flowed from
seven niches, originally framed by
tabernacles with columns in antique
yellow marble set upon purple marble
platforms and embellished by statues.
From the collecting basin at the foot
of the niches, the water was fed into
the fountains of the central chamber,

and then flowed into the long central
basin and the minor fountains of the
garden. To the sides of the chamber,
two small courtyards led to different
spaces that were covered by barrel
vaults, arranged according to
a symmetrical scheme. The function
of this pavilion is still uncertain.
The central chamber has been
interpreted as a *coenatio*, while more
recently, on the basis of a comparison
of the entire Piazza d'Oro complex
with the Stoa of Hadrian in Athens,
the hypothesis that this was the
emperor's private library has
been advanced.
Along the eastern side of the garden
is another series of spaces, not well
preserved, that include a small
apsidal room, a rectangular space
paved with a mosaic of crude
manufacture with three niches on
one of the long sides, and an ample
semicircular room. The latter is
characterized by a vaulted ceiling
and niches on the rear wall from
which water flowed into an ellipsoid
basin nearby; this chamber has
been identified as a summer *coenatio*,
according to an organizational
scheme analogous to that of the
Serapeum. Several latrines were
located between the walls. Adjacent
to this chamber was another
complex of spaces, with *opus sectile*
floors that are poorly preserved.
On a lower level, toward the valley,
was an arena for gladiatorial games
which is also poorly preserved, as
well as, perhaps, a stadium, a marble
model of which, recovered inside
the villa, is displayed in the Didactic
Museum. Near the space with the
polychrome mosaic is the entrance to
the *cryptoporticus* that runs along the
northern side of the Piazza d'Oro and
joins the subterranean road at a right
angle. The segment of road along the
eastern side of the complex leading

Ephesus type statue of Hera.

Reconstructed plan of the complex.

to the Large Trapezium could accommodate horses and carriages. The kinds of spaces, the presence fountains, the exclusive use of *opus sectile* in all the floors of this edifice—with the exception of the two spaces on the sides of the Vestibule, which, however, bore an elaborate mosaic, and the rectangular room near the *triclinium*, paved with a crude mosaic due to the fact that it had no roof—and, finally, the widespread use of marble wall facing, known only through the holes in the brick walls, confirm the hypothesis that this area of the villa was closely connected to the public functions of the palace, even though it is set in a somewhat isolated position.

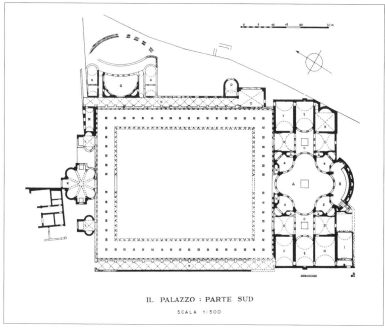

IL PALAZZO : PARTE SUD

SCALA 1:500

The Guard Barracks

Erected during the first phase of the villa's construction, when it seemed to be situated in a rather marginal area of the property, compared to the location of the Imperial residence, this multi-level building, set symmetrically around a central courtyard, is generally identified as the lodging space for the body of guards who oversaw the security of villa; the structure can be compared to the Guard Barracks in Ostia. This was unquestionably a service structure, as indicated by the *opus spicatum* pavement in the courtyard and the spaces on the first floor, as well as the prevalent use of wood for stairs and the floors of the other spaces that faced onto the galleries. Recently, scholars have postulated that this was the palace's kitchen and storage area, but its position and the presence of a guard house and latrines on the western side would appear to favor the more common hypothesis. While this is a rather modestly furnished building, that fact that it is free-standing suggests that it was not reserved for servants and slaves, who would have slept in the underground spaces attached to the villa, as, for example, in the case of the Hundred Chambers.

The Latrines

Beginning by at least the 2nd century BC, public latrines of rather monumental stature were built in the city of Rome, which substituted the very rudimentary facilities consisting of reutilized terracotta recipients (for example, amphorae whose tops had been cut off to provide a wider aperture), that were located along the streets and served as urinals. The new kind of latrine, which we later see in Imperial bath complexes and which at Hadrian's Villa is exemplified by the facilities in the Hospitalia, the Guard Barracks, the spaces along the western side of the Canopus, and the Hundred Chambers, consisted of a rectangular space furnished with a stone or marble bench that generally ran along three sides of the chamber and were perforated by regularly spaced holes, whose number was determined by the number of people who frequented the spaces. Ancient toilet habits were quite different from those of our civilization, which for us involve privacy. Thus, Roman latrines were conceptualized to be used contemporaneously by more than one person. Only under exceptional circumstances, as in some of the buildings in Hadrian's Villa, such as the Maritime Theater, the Tempe Pavilion, the Piazza d'Oro, the Winter Palace, the Canopus, and Roccabruna, were single latrines installed. These were evidently used by the emperor and his court, as the remains of marble faced walls and floors confirm. Below the seating platform was a sewage channel that was supplied with a constant flow of water for the continuous removal of waste from the conduits of the residential spaces. At the foot of the perforated bench was often another small channel where water also flowed, which may have been used to dip a sponge attached to a rod that was used for personal hygiene, a custom reported to us in the ancient sources.

Building with a Fish Pond

Column and capital.

This structure, consisting of two contiguous bodies along the side overlooking the Nympheum-Stadium was arranged on three levels, connected internally by a set of stone stairs. The middle floor contains rather modest spaces and the ceilings are notably lower, while the corridors are very narrow. Researchers postulate that this was a service area which, when completed, hosted a *praefurnia*. The principal

characteristic of the structure is, in fact, that almost all of the rooms on the upper floor were furnished with *suspensurae*. It is also possible that the rooms on the lower floor, which appear to have been raised in respect to the Nympheum-Stadium, were provided with a system of *suspensurae*, therefore providing a source of heat. For this reason, the building has been named the Winter Palace. Considering the dominant position of the edifice, compared to the surrounding buildings, its centrality within the estate and the rich decoration of the walls and floor which were faced in marble, today only reconstructable based upon the impressions left in the wall plaster and the holes in the wall where pegs were inserted, it would appear that this truly was the emperor's residence, that could even be used during the winter, given the provision of a heating system. This structure contains all the features required of an Imperial residence: monumental public areas as well as a series of minor spaces, a peristyle and *cryptoporticus* in order to walk beneath the sun or in the shade, according to the season and a large garden with dining areas for the summertime, recognized in the adjacent Nympheum-Stadium. Like most of the buildings in the Imperial Palace, the lavish nature of the complex inspired treasure hunters to strip all the marble furnishings from the walls and floors, as well as the columns and other architectural members over the centuries in order to decorate their own new palaces. However, although only the skeleton of this building remains today, it is still possible to appreciate the impressive size of the interior spaces and, in particular, the enormous chamber that overlooks the

Signature of Piranesi on the vault of the *cryptoporticus* with the Fish Pond.

Nympheum-Stadium that was probably used for banquets or ceremonies during the winter. From here, one could see the garden of the Pecile and gaze onto the countryside that led toward Rome. In a more remote position within this complex was an area characterized by a large raised platform flanked by columns, that may have served as an audience hall. Nearby, on the south side, were private latrines, situated in the spaces between the pillars that supported the cross vault of an apsidal space. To one side of the residential zone was the so-called Fish Pond, a large rectangular pool adorned by a cycle of statuary, indicated by the presence of regularly spaced niches along the edge and surrounded by an ample portico with Corinthian columns that was paved in *opus sectile*. Between the portico and pool was an exclusively functional corridor, set somewhat lower, that was not roofed and was paved with a mosaic. Along the external sides of this sunken space were forty splayed windows, conveniently protected by the edge of the roof over the colonnade that provided air and light to the subterranean gallery. This gallery, located beneath the portico and accessible by means of a still functional stone stairway faced with white marble, consists of four wings completely faced in plaster. On the preserved section of the plaster are the signatures of modern visitors and famous artists, such as Piranesi. The notable quantity of earth that once filled the *cryptoporticus* and was slowly emptied is the reason why the inscriptions, often bearing the year and the visitor's city of origin, are found on the summit of the vaults as well as on the walls.

79

Nympheum-Stadium

Defined as a Stadium until the excavations in the 1950s, on account of its aggregate form, this area is actually a large garden with fountains and pavilions, which stands before the Building with a Fish Pond on the side of its principal entrance. Connected directly, to the north, with the Pecile, the Baths with Heliocaminus as well as, on the other side of the subterranean passageway, with the Maritime Theater and the Philosophers' Chamber and, to the south, with the *Quadriporticus* in front of the Small Baths, the main entrance into the Nympheum-Stadium was through the Building with Three Exedras. In line with the central covered room of the latter building was a courtyard, probably filled with plants, that was flanked by porticoes through which one could reach the Building with a Fish Pond on the opposite side of the courtyard. Apart from serving as a communication hub between the various areas of the villa, this space also functioned to separate the two wings of the Nympheum-Stadium, that were arranged in different ways. The northern wing consists of a vast rectangular garden with a portico,

onto which three spaces opened—the central area contained a raised niche where a statue would have been set that was visible from a distance—and probably, at the extremity, a latrine. The garden was furnished with a long rectangular pool next to which two large flower pots of the same size were set and are still visible today. This was followed by an area bordered by pillars, that may have supported an arbor, with a square fountain at the center and six hexagonal fountains of smaller dimensions on the exterior. Finally, near one of the porticoes in the central courtyard and opening onto it, was a pavilion (destroyed, like the majority of buildings in the surrounding area) surrounded by walls and columns. Scholars are still uncertain as to the kind of roof used to cover this structure. On the opposite side, set in a large fountain in the form of a stepped exedra with

Ionic capitals in white and gray marble.

Group of Niobes in gray marble.

Chiaramonti Niobe in white marble. Vatican City, Vatican Museums.

Running Niobe in gray marble. Vatican City, Vatican Museums.

a central niche and small waterfalls that must have created an impressive effect, was a large rectangular podium surrounded by columns. The location of this complex, which overlooks the monumental fountain and central courtyard, has led researchers to postulate that this served as a Summer Triclinium, which was probably only closed by curtains and whose floor was paved with a rich display of marble. This chamber is analogous to examples that already existed in Rome, such as the Auditorium of Mecenate, which was transformed into a Summer Triclinium, perhaps by Tiberius, and is also characterized by an apsidal plan with a stepped *cavea* and spouting water.

Small Baths

Exterior view, toward the Vestibule.

The facade, oriented toward the north, bears three niches that were originally framed by columns and was built in the *opus reticulatum* technique: this is a clear example of the reuse of a pre-Hadrianic construction. The orientation of the facade prefigured the entire plan of the complex, which is quite unusual. From the front of the building, a corridor led to the various areas of the baths through an octagonal chamber whose marble faced walls were alternately concave and flat; the ceiling consisted of a dome, while the floor, raised upon a system of *suspensurae*, was paved in a sumptuous manner with *opus sectile*, as the impressions of the small marble fragments in the concrete foundation indicate. The wealth and variety of the marble employed and the ornamental motifs that characterized all of the floors

in this edifice are exemplified by the still visible remains in one of the two corridors on the eastern side of the complex as well as in a small contiguous space that communicated with the octagonal chamber. Also in direct communication with the octagonal chamber and also heated is the circular chamber, or tholos, with a hemispherical dome and central oculus, which served as the *sudatio*. The other heated spaces were aligned on the same side of the complex, including the notably large room with short convex walls. The collapse of the floor, due to weaknesses in the system of *suspensurae*, brought to light the conduits through which hot air generated by the *praefurnia* circulated, while the stripping of the marble wall facing revealed the *ascensiores*, or vertical ducts through which vapor was channeled

Interior of the octagonal room.

outside the edifice. At the center of the complex is the *frigidarium*, with two large opposing basins embellished by sheets of white marble, accessible by means of steps faced in the same quality of marble. Behind this chamber, along the side that is set at a lower level is what is believed to be a gymnasium, arranged according to the plan utilized in the nearby Grand Baths. Despite the name, the Small Baths represent one of the most luxurious parts of the villa. Aside from the variety of the marble decoration, there is an incredible richness in the architectural design of the various spaces within the complex: in the vaults and the extraordinary efforts made to link pitched roofs and domes in a playful manner that alternated curves and lines. Therefore, this complex is evidently an important component of the Palace and, considering the close proximity to the Building with a Fish Pond, must have been used by the emperor.

Grand Baths

**Column in
cipollino marble
and Ionic capital
in white marble.**

The name of this complex
is derived from the spaciousness
of the individual chambers and
the large surface area compared
to the other baths of the villa.
The Small and Grand Bath
complexes were connected on
the western side by a subterranean
corridor that provided access
to the *praefurnia* and could be easily
approached by the service personnel
who resided in the area of the
Hundred Chambers. The heated
spaces of the baths were situated

along this side, among which,
immediately recognizable by its
circular form and the dome with a
central oculus as well as the absence
of pools, is the *sudatio*: still an
impressive sight today, despite the
collapse of the front section where
the large windows that captured
sunlight opened. This was followed
by the *tepidaria*–heated chambers
that had *suspensurae* beneath the
floor and, in some cases, terracotta
pipes or conduits for the circulation
of hot air—and the *caldaria*, the
spaces reserved for hot baths. The
central area is almost completely
occupied by the *frigidarium*, a large
rectangular chamber with a cross
vaulted ceiling, in which two pools
were set at a lower level. These
basins for cold plunges, one apsidal
and the other rectangular, were
accessible by means of steps,
embellished in marble, while
their entrances were framed by tall
columns of *cipollino* marble with
highly refined Ionic capitals. The
apsidal pool was originally adorned
by statues, as the presence of niches
in the rear wall suggest. From the
frigidarium one could enter, apart
from the circular sudatio, a large
chamber that was also heated,
located on the southern side, which
presents a peculiar feature consisting
of a ceiling decorated in stucco
with geometric motifs and figured
medallions, traces of which are
preserved in the pendentive corners
of the vault. On each side of the
rectangular basin was a corridor
that led to another rectangular space
with a mosaic floor, interpreted by
some scholars as a *sphaeristerium*
(area for playing ball), adjacent
to the gymnasium, that consists of
a spacious courtyard paved in *opus
spicatum* surrounded by a portico
with a mosaic floor; the columns

have not survived. The *opus spicatum* technique was also employed above the roof of the rectangular pool in the *frigidarium*, which evidently served as a terrace, as can be deduced by an examination of the collapsed blocks visible on the floor of the basin. This bath complex, too, demonstrates a notable variety

The Baths

The presence of three bath complexes within the confines of the villa should not be too surprising if we consider the fact that most Romans of every social class frequented baths on a more or less daily basis and that, since Hadrian's Villa was the official residence of the emperor, there must have been a great number of courtesans, guests, guards and servants who stayed on the premises of the villa at any given time. This number does not include the craftsmen involved in the ongoing construction of the various buildings and the installation of decorative and sculptural features in interior spaces and in gardens. The use of baths was a response to the norms of hygiene, dictated by medical treatises which prescribe the heating of the body in order to dilate pores through physical exercise and hot water. This was to be followed by immersions in warm water and, finally, a plunge into a basin of cold water. All bath complexes consisted of an *apodyterium* (dressing room), *laconicum* (sauna), *caldarium* (hot bath), *tepidarium* (warm bath) and *frigidarium* (cold bath), in addition to the gymnasium and other minor spaces. The great number of people who utilized the public baths must be considered in light of the fact that although all Roman cities were furnished with running water, the upper stories of common buildings were not supplied with water; therefore, the tenants residing in *insulae* (apartment buildings) were compelled to resort to the public baths. But it was not only the commoners who frequented these baths. Even the very wealthy who often had private baths in their homes regularly entered the large public complexes, because bathing was a very social event and many of the commercial and political agreements, as well as relationships with friends were conducted in these areas. Within the public baths, there were often separate quarters for men and women, or else the two genders entered the baths at different hours of the day, although promiscuity must not have been a rare event, if worried legislators were forced to order that men and women must not bathe simultaneously so many times throughout Roman history. Spartianus reports that Hadrian himself passed a law on this regard. Analogous to the best modern gyms, furnished with services that include swimming pools and areas for physical exercise, as well as specialists in massages and personal aesthetics, Roman baths were also highly complex institutions: apart from the pools containing water with different temperatures, there was the gymnasium which consisted of a courtyard where sports were practiced. This area was surrounded by a portico that was often embellished by statues and other works of art representing athletic subjects. There were also a series of minor spaces for massages, hair removal and other activities dedicated to the maintenance of the body. The public baths generally contained latrines that often lacked private stalls, as well as shops where a variety of services were offered: barbers, small restaurants, wine dealers, and other vendors where goods could be purchased. All the services were for payment, but the state imposed strict price limits for certain facilities and services, such as the use of toilets; thus, bath owners had to find other means, such as renting shops, in order to gain a sufficient economic return on these expensive enterprises. One needs only consider the costs involved in providing water for all the pools and the supply of wood required to heat the numerous spaces; there was also the problem of maintenance, that included the frequent changing of water in the pools, which was rigorously controlled.

Praetorium

of innovative architectural solutions, especially in the roofing system, which is quite monumental; however, the embellishments are not as sumptuous as the other baths of the villa. If one excludes the large chamber with the stucco decoration and the adjacent room with an *opus sectile* floor, the decorative scheme of this complex is somewhat more modest. The floors, largely preserved, are of white mosaic bordered by one or two black bands, while the walls were faced with plaster and not marble, a characteristic that has led researchers to hypothesize that this edifice was frequented by the servants residing in the villa.

Identified many years ago with the dwelling space reserved for the praetorian guards who served to protect the emperor, this edifice consists of just two bodies that are quite distinct from one another. The lower part is arranged upon three floors which are divided into a series of small spaces that do not communicate with each other, but were accessible by means of external walkways and sets of cement stairs, still visible at the western end. The wooden floors were supported by travertine corbels. The construction scheme is analogous to that of the Hundred Chambers and other service areas throughout the villa, which has led scholars to speculate that this building was used for the servile staff of the palace as well as a storeroom for alimentary goods. In this case, too, the humble dwelling spaces served as the substructure for the upper portion of the complex, a pavilion decorated with brick pilaster strips that connote the noble area of the complex.
In addition to the elevated position, the same level as the Building with a Fish Pond, this is confirmed by the accessibility to the nearby spaces of the palace.
Between the Praetorium and the Grand Baths is a sequence of spaces with frescoed walls bearing simple bands and panels, furnished with latrines—and, thus, interpreted as lodging space. Recently, scholars have proposed that the craftsmen who worked on the decorative program of the villa resided here. In fact, a large quantity of marble chips and other associated rubble has been found in this area as well as the white marble model of the stadium, now in the Didactic Museum.

The Canopus

This complex is one of the only features of the entire villa that can be identified with great confidence to one of celebrated areas described by Helius Spartianus in the *Vita Hadriani*. Constructed in a narrow artificial valley, this structure was bordered by masonry buttresses and its principal feature is a large body of water, that terminates with a highly decorated pavilion. This is the Canopus, whose name was borrowed from the canal that linked Alexandria to the city on the Nile delta bearing the same name. This area was renowned for the nighttime parties that occurred here. The large pool of water (119 × 18 meters), situated at the center of the valley, with the short, curved, northern end enhanced by a mixed architectural scheme, was bordered to the east by a double colonnade that supported an arbor, as the presence of vertical sheets of marble between the column bases suggest. A strip of garden was aligned with the colonnade. To the west, the sequence of columns along the pool was substituted by caryatids

and was probably connected (by another arbor?) to the retaining wall, discovered during the excavations along the artificial mound of earth on this side of the valley. The complex terminates with a monumental nympheum in the form of an exedra, called the Serapeum (from the temple of Serapis, located in the city of Canopus) and characterized by a dome that was originally decorated by a glass paste mosaic, and with a long uncovered apse to the rear. To both sides are a pair of minor structures that flank a rectangular pool in front of the nympheum. This was a large *coenatio*, as the presence of a *stibadion* (semicircular stone bench with an elevated surface), or banquet couch indicates, that, on the basis of its orientation toward the north of the complex and the presence of gardens, pools with small waterfalls and running water obtained by means of a complex pumping system on the dome that allowed a sheet of water to fall in front of the diners, was used during the hot

summer months. This area was the
focus of systematic excavations only
relatively recently, in the 1950s.
This archaeological work revealed
the *Euripus*, whose specific location
within Hadrian's Villa had not been
previously identified, and a lavish
series of marble statues, reliefs and
various types of decorative elements,
that constitute the largest body
of statuary known from a single
location in the context of
the villa. Knowing their exact
position in the archaeological
record and, hence, their
original location within
the Canopus, scholars have
formulated an idea, perhaps
imperfect, of the sculptural
program conceived by
Hadrian for this area.
The collection generally
consists of Roman copies
of Classical Greek original
statues, larger than life size,
among which are the four
maidens-caryatids (statues
that served to support
the trabeation), replicas
of the *korai* from
the Erechtheon on
the Athenian Acropolis
(end of the 5th century
BC), that were positioned

along the eastern edge of the pool.
Their discovery has allowed art
historians to precisely reconstruct the
appearance of the Greek originals,
whose arms are no longer preserved.
The *korai*, in turn, were flanked by
a pair of *sileni* holding baskets: the
basket of fruit substitutes the capital,
a form derived from Hellenistic
models originating in Alexandria.
The statues that embellished the
mixed architecture at the end
of the semicircular *Euripus*
represented a young warrior wearing
a tall helmet, the so-called "Ares,"
actually Hermes, recognized by the
caduceus, a typical attribute of the
god, traces of which are apparent
on his right arm, and two wounded
Amazons, reproductions of the
prototypes created
by Polyclitus and
Phidias for the
Temple of

Artemis at Ephesus. Even in the case of the Phidian Amazon, the example at Hadrian's Villa constitutes the most complete copy known to us from the ancient world and, although it is not entirely preserved, has allowed researchers to reconstruct a composite sketch of the Greek original: conceived as a standing figure who leans upon a spear, in order to compensate for her weakness caused by a wounded leg. Also derived from the excavations around the *Euripus* and, thus, belonging, with all probability, to the decorative cycle along the edge of the pool, even though we are unsure as to its precise position, are the personifications of the Nile and the Tiber, identified by the presence, respectively, of a sphinx and the she-wolf with Romulus and Remus. From the same area is a crocodile carved from *cipollino* marble, a variety of stone whose veins are particularly suitable for reproductions of this animal's skin: the presence of a lead pipe between the animal's jaws indicates that this was part of a fountain. It is very likely that the crocodile was situated on one of the two stone foundations discovered within the *Euripus*, possibly the northern one. Set upon a platform to the south was a large, hemispherical base in marble, still *in situ*. Recovered on the ground were hundreds of fragments of the same kind of marble, evidently part of a sculptural group originally positioned on the platform immediately below the sheet of water, as if they were emerging from the depths of the channel. The lower part of the foundation still preserves the original decoration with different kinds of marine animals between the waves, while the fragmentary medallion bears a scarcely recognizable bare chested female

Amazon.

Amazon.

figure; the lower portion of her body blended into a group of dogs and fishtails. This is a representation of Scylla, the sea monster described in the *Odyssey* as a ferocious eater of the seamen who accompanied Ulysses on his journeys. Of the surviving fragments, at least two male figures can be discerned, both in the process of being devoured by the dogs and restrained by the twisted fishtails. A reconstruction of the group with marble copies of the originals created by the German sculptor H. Schröteler

(1916–1999) through the study of many other fragments housed in various museums (Vatican, Rome, Palermo and Berlin) presents an idea as to the overall sculptural composition. The vivid representation of Scylla's body, which emerges from the frenzied circle of dogs and fishtails like a terrifying apparition as the dogs tear the defenseless victims apart, is striking. The violent torsion of Scylla and the drama of the scene, which inspires pathos in viewers, together to the pyramidal form of the group, recall Hellenistic models. The

Egyptianizing statues carved in basalt, antique red marble and granite, some of which depict Antinous with the characteristic hooded *nemes* and the folded girdle were discovered in the area of the Canopus in the 18th century and are currently housed in the Vatican Museums. On the other hand, the scarce documentation pertaining to the recovery of these statues by Jesuit priests, at the time when the land encompassing Hadrian's Villa was owned by this order, does not reveal the findspots with certainty or the original

organization of the sculptural program in the so-called Serapeum, that some scholars have reconstructed on the basis of a celebration of Antinous, who Hadrian divinized after the youth's death under mysterious circumstances in the waters of the Nile in AD 130, is the subject of heated discussion. Numerous Egyptian and

disposition of the individual pieces of sculpture. The presence in this context of portraits of Antinous with a cobra protome on his hood, that liken him to pharaohs with the evident allusion to the divinization of Hadrian's young companion, may support the hypothesis that the edifice was restored in honor of Antinous; after all, Hadrian dedicated

Scylla,
reconstruction
by H. Schröteler.
Bochum, Ruhr
Universität,
Kunstsammlungen.

temples and, even, an entire city to
Antinous (Antinoopolis), during the
emperor's return voyage from Egypt,
i.e., after AD 133–134. Based upon
brick stamps (dated to AD 123–124)
scholars know that the Canopus
was originally constructed in the
first building phase of the villa, even
though some examples discovered

in the ground near the *Euripus* bear
later dates, indicating a continuation
of work. These brick stamps date
no earlier than AD 125–127, and
occur far less frequently than the
earlier examples found on bricks still
in their original position in the walls
of the structure and in the earthen
fills around the same area.

Terracotta vases recovered in the Canopus garden.

Young Hadrian.

If we accept the hypothesis of a later transformation of the building, there is still the problem regarding the decoration of the first phase. The heads of three male subjects discovered in the 18th-century excavations conducted by G. Hamilton in the Pantanello marsh have been identified with Ulysses' companions from the famous group representing the blinding of the Cyclops. That such a cycle was present at Hadrian's Villa is partially based upon the fact that another similar group is known from Tiberius's villa in Sperlonga. Scholars believe that the large nympheum of the Serapeum was a privileged location within the villa, with its artificial grotto, emphasized by the presence of a fountain that was installed into a niche made of pumice stone. The lateral niches would have hosted other statues related to the same subject, as other cases attest. Until now no sufficient proof has been demonstrated to support the various hypotheses that attempt to explain the sculptural program of the Serapeum and its significance— the same is true for the spaces situated in the lateral wings—thus, the question still lies open. The pavilion of the Canopus also included natural areas, arranged as gardens, which were also adorned with statues and relief sculpture carved in many kinds of marble, demonstrated by the discovery of small pillars, vases, the legs of tables, masks of Bacchus, and theatrical masks on the fountain, all elements that routinely characterized the Roman garden. Because early "archaeologists" did record the details regarding the precise findspots of "minor" pieces of art and their archaeological context, modern researchers are unable to reconstruct the disposition of the various sculptural elements that would allow them to gain an understanding of the concepts followed in the planning of the gardens at Hadrian's Villa. Recent archaeological campaigns aimed specifically at the organization of the gardens at the villa have shed considerable light on the location of shrubs and flower beds as well as their relationship with the fountains and pools that complemented the gardens and peristyles. Furthermore, at the foot of the slope along the eastern side of the *Euripus*, archaeologists uncovered a long flower bed that ran parallel with the edge of the pool and contained rows of terracotta flower pots; the pots were of various dimensions, but each vessel bore characteristic holes on the wall and the floor. The intentional placing of holes in the pots served to allow the roots to enter the surrounding earth, suggesting that they were provisional. As the roots of the various species of plants reached their maximum dimensions and there was less of a need for the arrangement of the pots in a decorative manner, for example after blossoming, the plants were either placed into larger pots or directly into the soil. Aside from using true flower pots, the gardeners of this epoch also reutilized transport amphorae, that were cut into an appropriate form and then perforated. Obviously, the upper

93

Garden around
the Canopus
during the
excavations.

portion of the amphorae were employed by turning it over, so that the narrow end fit into the ground like its sawed-off base. Because of this practice, archaeologists have been able to date the organization of this garden to the era of Hadrian, on the basis of the types of amphorae recovered through the excavations. In addition to the ceramic evidence, maker's marks preserved on some bricks also point toward a date during the first decades of the 2nd century AD. The work is attributed to a group of Libyan workers.

Antiquarium of the Canopus

When the archaeological work in area of the Canopus brought so many pieces of sculpture to light that embellished the *Euripus*, a decision was made to replace the original statues with exact copies, created immediately after the discovery of the originals in order to protect the ancient marble. The originals were to be housed in a closed space, preferably in close proximity to their findspots. Administrators chose a location on the substructures of the western terrace for the future museum. The ancient structures underwent heavy modifications: the interior spaces were made to communicate with a sequence of parallel apertures and were paved with fragments of the different types of marble found throughout the villa, assembled according to the tastes of the era. This caused serious damage upon the Roman structure, but an even more negative result was the complete obliteration of the space between the foundation wall of the substructure and the retaining wall of the earthen fill, which led to an alteration in the internal microclimate. A notable increase in humidity occurred that compromised not only the walls of the structure, but the original statues on display, as well. In recent years, it became necessary to undertake a program of restoration throughout the edifice, to stabilize the lower portion, damaged by humidity, and to salvage the upper level of the substructure, which had already been partially transformed in the 18th century into a Casa Colonica (farmhouse). These efforts also provided the opportunity to rearrange the display of the sculptures, whereby the cycle of statuary from the Canopus and a series of Imperial portraits from various sectors of the villa were relocated onto the uppermost floor. This relocation to the upper story, consisting of three airy spaces that overlook the central pool of the Canopus, provided a far more adequate context for the works of statuary, which were now placed closer to their original findspots. The gallery on the lower floor contains examples of the architectural decoration and minor decorative elements, as well as samples of the wall facing and flooring that characterize the opulent tastes of Hadrian. Situated near the cycle of statuary from the Canopus and a series of other sculptural works from different areas of the villa are also a number of portraits recovered in the 20th-century excavations of the *Euripus*. These include a portrait of the young Hadrian, that represents the only image of the emperor still in Hadrian's Villa, and one of Julia Domna. The latter example, together with the bust of Lucius Verus from the Pantanello marsh and those of Crispina, Septimius Severus and Caracalla, attest to the use of the villa as an Imperial residence at least until the Severan dynasty in the early 3rd century AD. Among the architectural elements and the samples of wall facing displayed are an important series of refined column bases and pilaster strip capitals in different types of marble. This wide variety of form and decoration, antefixes in white marble, fragments of frescoes, stucco and elements of wall facing in *opus sectile*, created with polychrome marble inlays set into a base of slate, confirm the exceptionally high level of quality craftsmanship, even of the minor decorative features.

The Art of Gardens

With the conquest of Greece and the establishment relationships with the East through a series of military campaigns, the Roman world witnessed the rise of the concept of the garden as an open space intended for the cultivation of flowers, in addition to the long established *hortus*, which served the strictly practical function of raising of produce for the home. The earliest examples of villas containing peristyles ornate with decorative plants occur in Rome at the beginning of the 1st century BC, while the notion of the "constructed" garden developed during the early Imperial age. In the most luxurious residences, large areas were reserved for the creation of monumental gardens, cared for by the *topiarius*, where plants and shrubs were placed into an architectural setting; only the kinds of plants that were most suitable for the overall decorative effect desired by the proprietor were selected. The design of gardens also involved the presence of sculpture of various kinds, placed among the greenery, populating the space with mythological personalities connected with the natural world (Pan, Dionysus, Silenus, satyrs and maenads), animals, decorated vases, basins, pillars carved with vegetal motifs and small animals hidden among the leaves. Adorned with fountains, nympheums, statues and reliefs, the gardens assumed highly elaborate appearances. In the case of cities, as with the well documented examples in Pompeii, there was the tendency to imitate the grand parks that characterized pleasure villas in substantially reduced forms. The peristyles, filled more and more by decorative sculpture, also began to be embellished by wall paintings that depicted gardens, enhancing the illusion of being immersed in nature. In Imperial residences, the search for ever more elaborate solutions often led to fairly radical modifications of the natural environment. For example, in his villa in Velletri, Caligula had a massive oak tree moved into a *triclinium* that could be enjoyed by fifteen dinner guests; in constructing his singular villa in Subiaco, characterized by a sequence of pavilions and nympheums overlooking the narrow gorge through which the Aniene river passed, Nero dramatically modified the flow of the river through the construction of dams and artificial lakes.

Pompeii, peristyle of the House of the Vettii.

Fragments
of a painting
with a garden
from the
Vesuvian area,
AD 20–40

following pages
Plan of
Hadrian's Villa
showing the
present layout
of the gardens
in relation
to the buildings.

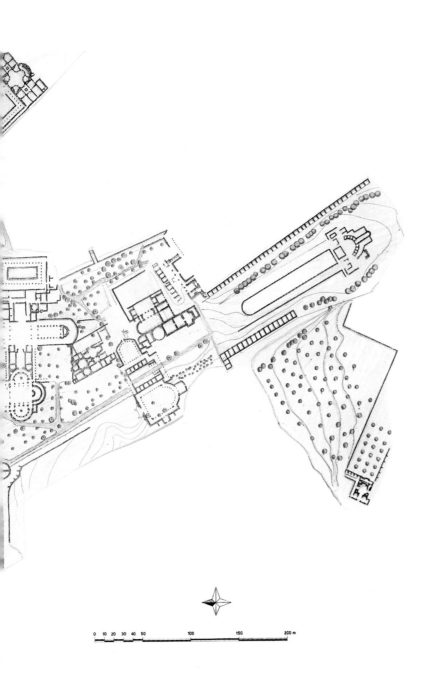

0 10 20 30 40 50   100   150   200 m

Pompeii,
House of the
Gold Bracelet,
triclinium.

Villa of Livia
at Primaporta,
underground
chamber.
Rome, Museo
Nazionale Romano
in Palazzo Massimo
alle Terme.

Torre di Roccabruna

The Vestibule

Situated in a remote area of the villa complex, at the western end of the Roccabruna olive grove, is a massive structure that some scholars claim was inspired by the celebrated Tower in the Accademia of Athens. This tower was composed of a parallelepiped with a square base upon which a cylindrical feature was placed that was surrounded by columns. Today, only the platforms of the epistyle bases, originally consisting of sixteen columns, are preserved. The upper region could be accessed by means of a ramp with inclined planes on an arched substructure, which can still be mounted. Judging from the massive walls, the tower was probably planned on three levels and served as a point from which the still beautiful Roman countryside could be admired. The terrace located above the vault of the central chamber consented a spectacular view of the hills around Tivoli as well as Rome and beyond.

The interior consisted of a large chamber—at the time paved in *opus sectile* with concentric bands of triangles, whose impressions in the cement undersurface are visible—as well as a series of minor spaces. A portico, added at a later moment of time, but completely fallen today, completed the structure.

This area was composed of a series of spaces and gardens that provided a way of passage between the Pecile and the Canopus and also connected with two of the thermal complexes, the Small and Grand Baths.

Still visible today is the garden area at the eastern end of the complex in the direction of the baths, and a portion of an elevated space that faced onto the paved road along the Hundred Chambers and bordered a porticoed area terminating with an exedra. From here, one could proceed through a number of minor spaces to a small temple that may have been dedicated to the family cult (*larario*), situated on the western side of the edifice.

In the lower level, the paved road continued through a subterranean passageway, articulated in several branches. The corridor, illuminated by splayed windows, connected the area of the Hundred Chambers directly with the corridor where the *praefurnia* of the Grand Baths was located and, by means of a secondary branch, with the Small Baths as well.

Recent archaeological research has revealed that on the side of the carriage road that skirted the Hundred Chambers there is a second paved road, located higher up. This road led to the entrance of the Vestibule, with a broad stairway, of which only the vertical foundation wall still remains, flanked by two niches set above fountains. These elements were already noted in 18th-century etchings, except for the access road that served as a monumental entrance to the villa, or at least one of the principal entryways. In fact, this was a one-way route beginning from the area corresponding to the junction with the Hundred Chambers, where

Building with Three Exedras

two architectural features can still
be observed that indicated the point
at which the road from via Tiburtina
assumed the form of a stadium,
in order to avoid the problems that
may have arisen if two vehicles
traveling in opposite directions
were to meet along this segment.
Along the side of the Hundred
Chambers, a wall that exists
in a fragmentary state, impeded
a view of the service area
from the Imperial residence.

This articulated complex is
composed of two wings: one is
characterized by a sequence
of open spaces; the other consists
of a series of heated spaces that
were embellished with precious
marble. This was another sumptuous
and monumental vestibule that led
into the Building with a Fish Pond,
the area that appears to have
been the private residence
of the emperor.
The portion of this structure
that faces the Pecile represented
the true atrium, which was
accessible from the wall to the
south of the large portico that was
interrupted by a doorway in front
of a large rectangular fountain,
creating a very large space framed
by columns. The heavy damage
suffered in recent centuries to this
section of the Pecile does not allow
the visitor to appreciate the effect
felt by people who arrived from
the portico, through the doorway
near the monumental fountain
surrounded by statues and columns,
beyond which one's vision was
guided toward a large statue set
in a niche, in a raised area at the
rear of an exedra in the garden.
With great ingenuity that resulted
from his exploration of innovative
architectural concepts, Hadrian
converted the atrium, occupied
entirely by the fountain, into an
impassable space, while the two
original lateral corridors assumed
the form of an entrance. The
fountain consists of a trapezoidal
structure that served as the cistern
that fed water to the fountain upon
which were three circular apertures.
The effect of the water, that gushed
upward, pouring into the channels
along the lower perimeter of the
cistern, was complemented by a rich
sculptural program, as twelve statue

Vescovali-Arezzo
type Athena.

Female dancer
from Tivoli.
Rome, Museo
Nazionale
Romano in
Palazzo Massimo
alle Terme.

bases situated around the basin attest. To one side is a broad rectangular space that was paved in marble—some scholars suggest that this covered chamber served as a summer *coenatio*—that overlooks the three exedras within a garden that gave the name to this complex. By passing through the easternmost exedra, characterized by a large door and two lateral niches, one could enter the principal area of the building's other wing, that ends with a rectangular niche bearing a large window. A series of rectangular cavities and dowel holes set at regular distances along the walls of this chamber suggest the presence of relief panels, mosaics, or other decorative elements that served to further embellish the walls, already faced with sheets of marble. Small doors located on the sides of the chamber that provided access to two groups of spaces arranged symmetrically, that opened onto the Nympheum-Stadium. The ceiling of this wing of the edifice was a flat terrace paved in *opus spicatum*, over which a crude mosaic composed of white *tesserae*, a type generally used for exteriors, was placed that is still visible on the fragments of the fallen ceiling within the spaces.

Capitals.

Column
and capital.

Nympheum and the Temple of Venus

Statue of Aphrodite of Knidos.

Detail of the upper part of the temple, with "laconian" type roofing.

Raised upon the substructures that overlooked the Tempe Valley, the Nympheum consisted of a semicircular plain, occupied at the center by a small temple aligned with the entrance. To the sides of the entrance, in perfect symmetry, were two apses with fountains, that mimicked the general form of the edifice. The circular plan of the central structure, the use of the Doric order and the discovery of a replica of the celebrated Aphrodite of Knidos led to the association between the Nympheum and the Greek tholos in Knidos, where the original statue by Praxiteles was located. The image of the complex, despite the restoration work conducted in the 1950s with the *anastilosis* of some columns and the trabeation, is incomplete, due to the 18th-century interventions for the construction of the Casino Fede, that was set upon the two apses of the Nympheum, incorporating portions into the later building and partially destroying other elements the structures. The former chapel located next to the casino hosted until very recently the statue

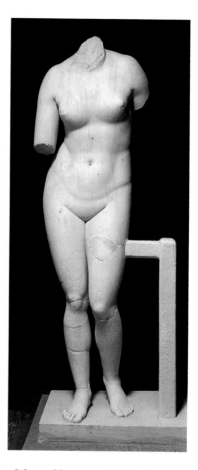

of the goddess, now displayed in the Antiquarium of the Canopus, while set inside the small temple, the probable original location of Aphrodite, is an exact reproduction. The precious *opus sectile* floors that presents different schemes in all of the areas of the Nympheum are still preserved *in situ*. The eastern side of the building's substructures consists of a series of niches separated by brick semicolumns and reutilizes an apsidal grotto from the Republican period, characterized by stalactites hanging from the vault and a large

Marble antefix, "laconian" type.

pool-*natatio*. The substructures also incorporate a paved road, once a Republican period path, employed as a passageway for carriages through the interior of the villa. The road, still partially preserved for a distance of about 40 meters, runs into a gallery covered by a barrel vault that is illuminated by rectangular apertures in the ceiling. On the undersurface of the vault are the impressions of wooden planks used to construct the frame over which the cement vault was thrown.

The Greek Theater

Despite its name, the Greek Theater
has the typical semicircular form of
a Roman theater and served, as its
position within the confines of the
villa and its reduced dimensions
suggest, as a small theater used
for performances before a select
number of spectators.
As with many other areas of this
monumental complex, the architects
took the topographic lay of the land
into account and adapted it to suit
the requirements of the structure.
In this case the natural outcrop
of tufa was exploited to create the
central portion of the *cavea*. The
exterior part of the *cavea* was set
upon vaulted substructures, that
were certainly employed as service
spaces. The stepped portion
of the *cavea* is still recognizable;
it is divided into two segments
by a central stairway, still partially
preserved. At the summit is a small

rectangular space which probably
served a sacred function: a small
temple is described by Pirro Ligorio
in the 16th century which, two
centuries later, was recorded on
Piranesi's map. At the foot of the
cavea, are the remains of the
orchestra, namely, the area where
the chorus was located during
tragedies and comedies, and the
proscenio, or stage, where the actors
performed. Rectangular in form,
only the lower section of the
proscenio is preserved. The remains
of the *frons scaenae* are no longer
visible, the fixed background built
in masonry generally arranged
on several stories and furnished
with numerous doors and windows,
that, besides delimiting the space
where theatrical works were
performed, was used for the scenic
backdrop. Of the two stairways
on either side of the *proscenio*,

**Etching of the
Greek Theater
by Jean-Honoré
Fragonard
(1732–1805).
Paris, private
collection.**

used by actors to enter and exit
scenes, only one remains.
It has been postulated that two
marble herms discovered during
the 18th-century excavations,
that represent personifications
of Tragedy and Comedy, now part
of the collections of the Vatican
Museums, were originally part
of the decorative program of the
theater. Nevertheless, this attribution
remains questionable, just like most
of the unprovenienced artifacts
discovered throughout the villa

in the oldest phase of excavation.
Adjacent to the Greek Theater
is, according to Piranesi's plan,
a rectangular building with a portico
bearing a retention wall with a
niches. Today only scant traces of
this edifice remain on the western
side of the theater.

Bibliography

The bibliography on Hadrian's Villa is extremely vast. Aside from the earliest publications, beginning with *Descrittione della superba et magnificentissima Villa Tiburtina* edited by Pirro Ligorio in the 16th century, the fundamental works are: H. Winnefeld, *Die Villa des Hadrian bei Tivoli*, Berlin 1895; P. Gusman, *La Villa Impériale de Tibur*, Paris 1904; H. Kahler, *Hadrian und seine villa bei Tivoli*, Berlin 1950; and S. Aurigemma, *Villa Adriana*, Rome 1961. Of the many recent publications, the titles listed here are among the most significant. A perusal of these works will lead the reader to the general bibliography of the villa, including references on the individual structures, architectural planning, and the programs of architectural decoration and sculpture that embellished the complex.

G. Lugli, "Villa Adriana," in *BullCom*, 55, 1927, pp. 139–204.
H. Bloch, *I bolli laterizi e la storia edilizia romana*, Rome 1947.
E. Salza Prina Ricotti, "Criptoportici e vie sotterranee di Villa Adriana," in *MEFRA*, 14, 1973, pp. 219–252.
C. Giuliani, P. Verduchi, "Ricerche sull'architettura di Villa Adriana," in *QuadTopRom*, VIII, 1975.
E. Salza Prina Ricotti, "Villa Adriana nei suoi limiti e nella sua funzionalità," in *RendPontAccRoma*, 51–52, 1978–1979, 1979–1980, pp. 237–294.
F. Coarelli, Lazio, Rome - Bari 1982, pp. 44–72.
J. Raeder, *Die statuarische Ausstattung der Villa Hadriana bei Tivoli*, Frankfurt a/M. - Berlin 1983.
H. Mielsch, *La villa romana*, Florence 1990 (Italian translation).
M. De Franceschini, *Villa Adriana. Mosaici, pavimenti, edifici*, Rome 1991.
Sectilia Pavimenta di Villa Adriana (edited by F. Guidobaldi), Rome 1994.
E. Calandra, *Oltre la Grecia. Alle origini del filellenismo di Adriano*, Perugia 1996.
W.L. MacDonald, J.A. Pinto, *Villa Adriana*, Milan 1998 (Italian translation).
Hadrien. Trésors d'une villa impériale, exhibition catalogue (edited by J. Charles-Gaffiot and H. Lavagne), Milan 1999.
Adriano. Architettura e progetto, exhibition catalogue, Milan 2000.

Photograph Credits

The photographs, from
the archives of the
Soprintendente Archeologica
per il Lazio, were taken
by Q. Berti and A. Briotti.

The plan on pp. 98–99 was
executed by S. Sgalambro.

The publisher is ready
to supply further information
on photographic sources
not mentioned to those
entitled to request it.

This volume was printed for Mondadori Electa S.p.A.
at Mondadori Printing S.p.A., Via Castellana 98,
Martellago (Venice) in the year 2004